Finding Your Passionate Purpose

In Life, Leadership, and Love

HEIDI MCKEE

WESTBOW
PRESS®
A DIVISION OF THOMAS NELSON
& ZONDERVAN

THE HOLY BIBLE, NEW INTERNATIONAL VERSION®,
NIV® Copyright © 1973, 1978, 1984, 2011 by Biblica, Inc.®
Used by permission. All rights reserved worldwide.

This book is a work of non-fiction. Unless otherwise noted, the author
and the publisher make no explicit guarantees as to the accuracy of
the information contained in this book and in some cases, names of
people and places have been altered to protect their privacy.

WestBow Press books may be ordered through booksellers or by contacting:

WestBow Press
A Division of Thomas Nelson & Zondervan
1663 Liberty Drive
Bloomington, IN 47403
www.westbowpress.com
1 (866) 928-1240

Because of the dynamic nature of the Internet, any web addresses or
links contained in this book may have changed since publication and
may no longer be valid. The views expressed in this work are solely those
of the author and do not necessarily reflect the views of the publisher,
and the publisher hereby disclaims any responsibility for them.

Any people depicted in stock imagery provided by Thinkstock are
models, and such images are being used for illustrative purposes only.
Certain stock imagery © Thinkstock.

ISBN: 978-1-5127-6245-7 (sc)
ISBN: 978-1-5127-6246-4 (hc)
ISBN: 978-1-5127-6244-0 (e)

Library of Congress Control Number: 2016918381

Print information available on the last page.

WestBow Press rev. date: 11/15/2016

For the ones that have shaped me, loved me, helped me pursue my passion, and believed in me. Marty, my love. Isaac, Rhea, Abby, for teaching me so much about myself. Mom, Dad, Grandparents, Nieces and Nephews for being my biggest fans. Sister Tammy, for your example, and My Besties- thanks for laughs, lessons and loving me through all my faults.

CONTENTS

PART 1 - Find your Passionate Purpose in Life 1

Chapter 1 Passion 3
Chapter 2 Purpose 8
Chapter 3 Uniqueness 15
Chapter 4 Personality 21
Chapter 5 Let's Go Europe 27

**PART 2 - Find your Passionate Purpose
in Leadership** 35

Chapter 6 That four letter word 37
Chapter 7 Consistency 45
Chapter 8 SERVANT LEADERSHIP 51
Chapter 9 Humility – eek! 59
Chapter 10 GOAL SETTING 65
Chapter 11 "Fake it 'til you make it!" 71
Chapter 12 BROKEN RECORDS 77

PART 3 - Find you Passionate Purpose in Love 87

Chapter 13 Love Language 89
Chapter 14 "Let's Get Married Then" 95
Chapter 15 Be Careful What You Wish For 103
Chapter 16 Undeserved Favor 110

Acknowlegments 119

Notes 123

About the Author 125

If you can't figure out your purpose, figure out your passion. For your passion will lead you right into your purpose." --Bishop T.D. Jakes

Finding your Passionate Purpose in

Life

Chapter 1

PASSION

"Light yourself on fire with passion and people will come from miles to watch you burn." --John Wesley

What is the first thing you think of when you hear the word passion? (please remember this is not one of *those* books). Does passion mean excited, loud, intense, really into it? I have been called passionate my entire life.

My coaches, my parents, my husband, and most recently my own kids and mentor have referred to me that way. They have all described me as a "passionate person". My husband goes on further – "Babe, you love passionately, you hate passionately … it must be exhausting being that passionate over everything." I'm not sure it is exhausting, but it has gotten me into a few binds.

When the dream of this book came into my mind I knew it was my calling to help others feel the passion of life I have and to give a glimpse of what living passionately looks like. In my opinion if you are not passionate about SOMETHING in your life, then you have a serious problem.

My desire is to help you see how living a life with passion can bring clarity to your existence, bring your relationships to a whole new level, and help you lead like you never have before.

One time I decided to go out after a football game my sophomore year in high school. There was a certain boy who wanted to bring me to the local taco shop and I thought it was a great idea. I'm really not sure if I was allowed to go, but I did anyway. (ask for forgiveness rather than permission-right?) When I came home, my father was waiting for me. My daddy – 5'10" with blonde hair, deep blue eyes and an oil roughneck who worked 24/7 – was a bit scary to my friends. A little rough around the edges, he put up an intimidating front.

We lived in a community where the houses were so close together that I knew when the neighbors went to the restroom because the light would shine into my room. It was a middle class, nice three-bedroom, two bath home with a pool – a typical suburban home.

We had this nice sectional couch that was placed right in the middle of the room. The couch was the only thing between my dad and me. "Where have you been young lady?" came spewing out of his mouth. I said something I shouldn't have, and in one leap – and when I say one leap, I mean like superman style – my dad jumped the sectional *and* coffee table and started after me in his boxer shorts.

For a split second I thought about apologizing, but then I saw it. I saw the Red Hot Passion coming out of my dad's eyes, and all I could do was run. I turned and ran out the door and down the street. I looked back once and saw my dad realizing he was in his underwear. I kept running. I have no idea what my father had planned on doing if he caught me. I just knew I deserved whatever he would bring.

My disrespect hurt him deeply. My haughty passion butted up against his angry fury. I realized that night my dad and I were quite similar. We had a deep belly kind of passion and if it was not directed correctly, he and I could both cause a lot of damage.

Passion to me is that feeling that you get when you JUST CAN'T hold back anymore. When the floodgates that were trying to hold it in, just bust open. Passion is not always bad! In fact, passion is very healthy and in many cases helped change the world.

Let me ask you a question. I really want you to think about this. This will help define your passion, or spark a potential passion in your life. Ok- here it goes.

IF MONEY WAS NOT AN ISSUE-AT ALL – I mean you don't need to make money, and you had as much as you needed to do whatever – what is one thing you'd get up and do everyday?

Ok, what was your initial response? Was it to have housekeepers? A drove of servants to wait on your every need? To go shopping all day everyday? If your first answer was somewhat superficial, as was mine, let's go a step further. Imagine if you did that thing EVERY SINGLE DAY for an entire year ... then what? WHAT would get you out of bed each morning?

I asked my Facebook friends what they would do. The answers were amazing! Many said they'd travel and see God's creation and see all the places they've only read about. Some said they'd do something meaningful for someone else – go on mission trips, build homes for the homeless, give generously, and care for the needy. Others mentioned things they love to do such as paint, scrapbook, read, dance, yoga. Most made mention of spending time with family, loved ones, and making memories.

Who knows what you came up with, but whatever it is, it's a start. Consider your answer. Maybe write it down. Dig through the layers. Find that area in your life that gets your belly stirring. Something that money can't buy, people can't give, or others can't influence. It's a YOU ONLY thing.

I know what my passion is. It's simple. It's one of the main reasons I decided to write this book. My passion is pushing people a little further then they ever thought possible. Encouraging others, believing in them, celebrating their victories, and coaching them to the next possibility. When I let the busyness of life distract me from my passion, I get cranky. And cranky, passionate people are NOT fun to be around.

As you read through the pages of this book, I will share personal stories of how I found my passionate purpose. We all have one! You have one, my children have one, even that homeless guy asking for money on the corner has a passionate purpose. Once you identify that God-given passionate purpose, that only you can have, life will start to be richer and you will feel so much more at peace. You will live fuller, love stronger, and lead more uninhibited. That is my goal-- For you, my friend, to find your passionate purpose and pursue it like a maniac!

Chapter 2

PURPOSE

"The two most important days in your life are the day you were born and the day you found out why." --Mark Twain

My mom is a saint. I have no clue how she has not one gray hair on her head. Raising me must have caused ulcers, migraines, prayer vigils – and who knows what else? By the time I was 5 years old, I had already been run over by a car, had massive surgery that left me in a cast for 12 months, and totaled a pickup truck with just me and my baby sister inside. If I were her, I'd be wanting a trade in by now. But she never did. She always kept an even pace that was consistent and purposeful.

Do you want to hear about the truck being totaled? Of course you do.

Remember, I told you my dad was an oil roughneck. That meant he worked on oil rigs. Sometimes all night and all day. We were living in Vernal, Utah at that time, when my dad had some time off. Being the kind of man he was, time off meant "Let's go get some work done". And that is what he did.

Dad, my mom, my 2-year-old baby sister and I all went up into the mountains to chop some firewood. I guess you can just go into the woods, cut down trees, and go burn the wood. When the chainsaw started up, my wise mom put us in the cab of the pickup, all safe and sound.

Unbeknownst to her, I knocked the gear-shift into neutral. She noticed the truck starting to roll. Panicking, she grabbed the tailgate to stop us rolling. Her heels dug into the ground and she immediately realized her inability to stop the rolling truck.

Can you imagine, knowing your babies are in a "run away" pick-up truck and there is ABSOLUTELY nothing you can do about it? She screamed at my dad and he jumped to the driver's side door. Of course it was locked. That's what passionate little girls do when they are scared. "Heidi, open the door!" he hollered as he was jogging along side the pickup as it gained speed going down this massive mountain. "Surely it will hit a tree and stop" my mom was thinking, trying hard not to panic.

About the time I actually got the door unlocked and open, a massive tree got in the way and my dad had to slam the door shut and run around the tree. At a full sprint now, he made one last leap and grabbed the door handle. It slipped out of his hand

and the truck ran him over. As he finally gathered himself and looked up, the truck flew off a 100-foot mountain.

As they both cried and ran to the side of the cliff, they saw the pickup smashed in two. "It was like a folded matchbook!" My mom remembered. "Every single window was shattered, and I knew you had been thrown from the cab." When my parents made it down the side of the mountain to the vehicle, they found my sister and I snuggled in the floorboard covered in broken glass, with not one scratch on our bodies.

You may not have a miraculous story like that, but if you are breathing, reading this with your eyeballs, able to understand these words, and have different emotions, then you have a miracle story.

Consider your conception (I know it may be gross thinking of your parents in that light). However, I mean the actual science of the whole deal. I am not a scientist, but let me try to break it down. The chances that your mom and your dad met, in this era- and all the family tree before them; then actually hookin' up; producing the exact sperm at the exact time that fertilized the exact egg to create you is (Are you ready for this?)!

1 in 10 to the 2.6 millionth power!
That is 10 with 2,685,000 zeroes behind it.

Consider it this way: If I put only zeroes (you being one of those) – single spaced – on every page of this book, front and back, it would take about 7,000,000,000,000 (yep-7 quadrillion) books with 500 pages of zeroes! The largest library in the world only holds 150 million volumes. That's a mere .0002%. Try finding one specific zero out of THAT many zeroes! Almost impossible right!?

Now's a great time to pause and take that in …

YOU- my friend-are a miracle!

You are – against the odds – that little zero that would be IMPOSSIBLE to find!

There is a reason you are alive and breathing today! Although the odds of finding your purpose may be just as staggering, by now you should be believing in miracles. I believe you have a purpose. My prayer is that you believe you have a purpose too.

This concept is best described in the life of George Bailey in "It's a Wonderful Life." The story is powerful, and although George was a simple man, with simple means, he had a purpose. His purpose was to show kindness and love to others.

What about Abraham Lincoln? Do you ever think of him without a beard? When he first started his political career he was clean shaven. A young girl sent him a letter recommending he grow whiskers so that he would look more mature. The iconic president was marketed by a young person with a purpose! So simple, yet so profound.

You may not influence a president, or lead massive revivals around the world, or earn a Nobel peace prize. But you may have a massive influence on someone that might!

Let's consider those closest around you. My parents constantly spoke affirmations over me. They taught me I can do anything. I was not the fastest, the smartest or the prettiest, but I never heard that from my parents. In fact, I heard things like, "You can do anything if you put your mind to it." "Try it Heidi, you never know, you may just accomplish it."

I have seen that with my own children. They hear everything I say. What if I say the word that will put their heart into motion to actually change the world one day? Or maybe the right words will impact a neighbor, coworker, in-law, or grocery store clerk?

As a direct-sales person, I conduct in-home parties. My friends gather together, I show them the cute things I'm selling, and we all have a good time eating, laughing and shopping in the comfort of someone's home. At one particular party, I decided to have all the guests say out loud what they love about the hostess—let's call her "Rene". As one by one shared, "Rene", my hostess started to squirm.

"She's a very good friend."

"She always welcomes me into her home."

"She's a great listener."

On and on the room filled with encouragement for this precious woman. We laughed, cried and shopped. The night was a blast. As I was packing up to go, I asked this sweet hostess what she thought about the party. After a long pause she looked up at me with tears streaming down her face. "I have never heard that many good things about me. In fact, I am in a horrible abusive marriage and for the last week I've been contemplating suicide."

It was clear that my purpose was to bring light into that hostess' life for that moment. To show her what a miracle her life is and that she too has purpose!

What is your purpose? Have you ever considered it?

The only way I know how to define purpose is in a spiritual sense. Without a good God/Creator – with eternity in the balance – there is no need for purpose, passion, breath. But that's an entirely different book. For the sake of time, I'm going to assume you believe in a higher power, a creator God who loves you beyond reason or comprehension.

In Rick Warren's best selling book Purpose Driven Life[1], he explains the five reasons we exist:

* We were planned for God's pleasure
* We were formed for God's family
* We were created to become like Christ
* We were shaped for serving God
* We were made for a mission

Just referring to these five points may be oversimplifying a tad … but the fact is you were made for a purpose!

Do you have an idea of what your purpose may be? What if you don't find it? No worries, beloved, we are in this together! Your purpose right now – right here – is to curl up, read this book and focus on you for just a moment! We will assess your gifts, we will overcome things holding you back, and I dare promise you will be finding a purpose before you know it!

---

[1] Warren, Rick <u>The Purpose Driven Life: What on Earth am I here for?</u> Grand Rapids, MI: 2009

Chapter 3

UNIQUENESS

"Why fit in when you were born to stand out." –Dr. Suess

In this day and age of technology, it seems that everyone wants to be like everyone else. My oldest daughter, at age 11, got caught up in "mean girl drama" this past school year. If you don't know what "mean girl drama" is, I'll give you a short version.

Mean girl situations occur when one girl wants to hurt another girl so she can fit in with still another girl. It's stupid and it's mean. My daughter didn't really want to be this girl's friend, but EVERYONE was her friend. If she didn't sit by her at lunch or play with her at recess, she would be called weird. So what if you are weird!? Getting that across to a child can be a challenge. When you're 11 years old – and weird – your life is pretty much over.

So when the opportunity came to bash and be bashed on social media, my daughter was caught right up in it! Instead of standing up and being her unique self, she folded into the envelope of being cool.

Why is it so wrong to be a little different? As we learned before, not only are you a true miracle to even be here right now, but you are utterly and completely unique! Out of the 5 billion people living today and 104 billion that have lived on earth throughout all of history, there's only one you. (Please do not quote me on that number – I did not do a census so I may be exaggerating for the sake of my argument). But the fact remains that out of a LOT of people there is not ONE like you! NOT ONE!

How in the world can there be so many variations?! It's mind boggling – there is NO ONE with your same DNA, NO ONE with your same footprint, fingerprint, breath, brain matter, or even the same personality.

WOW! This blows my mind. We are completely and 100% unique – bonafide- one-of-a-kind special!

Let's think about this for just a moment. Look at that freckle on your arm. Yep, the one on your right arm near the elbow … rest assured that NO ONE on earth has one just like it in the exact same place or in the same shape. And consider your hair follicles. NO ONE on earth or who has lived on the earth has the same hair follicle make-up as you do! The way you laugh, smile, cry, snore is unique. Although we may have similarities, there is NO ONE on earth who is just like you! You are set apart! You are different! You are unique! You are YOU!

Have you ever been to one of those "paint and sip" kind of places? They are a hit around here. It's a place where you go and drink wine while you paint on a giant canvas. The basic idea is to get everyone feeling so good about themselves that they paint freely, and by the end, they think their picture will sell for millions!

Most of the time, the group will show up and the instructor will give directions on what to do. First she will start with the sketching of the picture. She'll make sure everyone has it just right in regards to the spacing, proportions and layout. Many times, she'll even sketch it out for you. After you've completed the sketch, she'll instruct you to paint the backdrop. Step by step, she helps you paint your masterpiece while you drink wine.

Keep in mind that everyone in the class had the same instructions, the same canvas to work with, the same brushes and the same paint and colors. But in the end, not one painting is exactly alike! They are all unique!

This is the same with you!

The Creator of the universe created you! Although you may be similar to others, there are more differences than there are likenesses! You may counter with "What about identical twins!?" They have the exact same genome, they are created with the exact same DNA, so how in the world can they be unique?

I'll attempt a scientific explanation – one last time – to hone in my point. Our brains are full of a bazillion neurons, give or take a few. Every second of every minute of your life, the neurons are shooting information back and forth all over your brain.

Depending on the exposure of outside stimulants the firing of these neurons and the information traveling back and forth will vary a great deal. Depending on the information traveling through, they will trigger certain genomes and neglect others.

It's 100% impossible to be exactly alike. With that many neurons firing and that many different variations on top of that many different outside sources, the outcomes are so varied there is no way two will be duplicated. Case closed, sweet friend. You are you and there is NO one else like you.

So why do we try so hard to be like everyone else? Some days I wish I could just go cut that wire. I wish we could be wired more like my sweet nephew Victor. He is privileged to participate in Special Olympics. (If you have never been, I recommend you attend one.) Victor and his colleagues are there simply to do their best.

In one particular race I watched, there were four boys running 100 meters. Some were super fast and some were not. The small redhead, dead last by about 20 yards, stopped right in the middle of the race and waved at his cheering fans. He continued on as fast as his little legs could go.

At the finish line he was celebrated the same – if not more – than the child who came in first! His smile was big and he received hugs, high fives and great applause. It made me think … why can't we just be happy running our OWN race at our OWN pace? Why do we feel the need to jump in someone else's lane?

Speaking of lanes, please let me share one more Special Olympics story. Six kids lined up to run a 200-meter dash, and when the starting gun exploded they all looked forward to making it to the finish line. Again, some runners were fast and some were not. In fact, the last runner labored to keep up the pace. He struggled every step of the way and my heart truly went out to him. Seconds passed, then minutes after everyone else passed the finish line, yet he still trudged on. There was unbelievable crowd participation and they cheered so loud that you couldn't hear yourself talk!

FINALLY, he crossed the finish line and the audience erupted. During the closing ceremony, this boy was the only one to receive a medal for that race. Not because he was first, but because he was the only participant to stay in his lane.

Maybe it's just me, but I seem to want to jump into my neighbor's lane. I want to run someone else's race, maybe because he's faster, more successful or has more peace! Whatever the reason, it's not right. We are unique and here for a purpose. Run your race, set your pace, until you see our Creator face to face.

Chapter 4

PERSONALITY

"Be you because everyone else is taken." --Author Unknown

One of the funniest and scariest experiences that ever happened to me took place about five summers ago. My immediate family, parents, sister and brother-in-law decided to go to the lake. My dad had a big 25-foot camper that slept six people, we borrowed a little pop up camper that slept five, and we also borrowed a boat. Clearly, we have some trusting friends! We had not gone on a family lake vacation in a very long time, so let's just say we were a little rusty on some of the "must haves".

Once we got our camp set up and the beds made, we launched the boat. This fun 19-foot ski boat comfortably holds 5-7 adults. With this all-inclusive boat, we were able to load all six adults, three kids and every toy we could find. Dad sported his captain's hat, the kids bunkered down in their very form-fitted life vests, my sister, mom and I were lathered with our sun screen, and we could not wait to get on the open lake with the wind in our hair.

We got about 100 yards from the dock and something just did not feel right. The boat was lagging and making an awful gargling noise. Even I knew something was weird … then we saw it … water in the boat! In fact, the floorboard was *covered* with water.

Oh my! – we were going down in our friend's boat, just like the Titanic. All of a sudden my dad remembered "Oh NO! THE PLUG! WE FORGOT THE PLUG!" He reached in the glove compartment (I'm not sure why you'd have a glove compartment on a boat) and pulled out the one-inch gold round thing that looks like you can screw it into a hole. I jumped up, grabbed the plug and dove in.

Mind you, I had NEVER screwed in a plug on a boat, let alone knew that boats even HAD plugs, but I was there to save the day. Gasping for air, I dove under the boat with panic in every fiber of my body. Popping up to ask where I should go, the excitement was overtaking me and I couldn't stay under long enough to find the hole – let alone screw in the plug. I tried – for what seemed like days – until finally my brother-in- law, like a dolphin playing in the waves, dove in, grabbed the plug and screwed it in

ALL IN ONE FELL SWOOP!

My daughters were crying (because obviously we almost died). My dad was white as a ghost, my sister was in the water too (because she thought she'd help me), my husband was sitting in the front just shaking his head, and my mom was counting all her little chickens to make sure we were all safe and sound.

Once the ordeal was over and we were able to bilge out all the water, we started to laugh. And I mean we laughed and laughed until we couldn't laugh any more. The way our personalities came to light was so funny and the adrenaline amplified them all the more.

In that time of desperation, I stepped up and wanted to take control (although I had no idea how). I was out of control, over excited, and just too dramatic to really get the job done. My sister, just as ill-equipped as I, jumped in to aid me. She has always been very supportive. My dad was yelling commands from the deck, knowing his boundaries, yet understanding the depth of the job. My husband retreated. He sat back and watched me make a fool of myself. My mother was coddling and loving on the poor babes abandoned by their mother, probably saying prayers and blessings over the boat. And my brother-in-law took a deep breath, assessed the situation, then calmly, with assurance, jumped in and saved the day.

When we reflect on this experience, we still crack up even today. We ended up buying that exact boat from those friends, and since then have purchased half a dozen plugs, just to be on the safe side! And every time we get in the boat someone exclaims, "Don't forget the plug!"

What a weird way to display our personalities! But it's so true! Sometimes in the heat of the moment, when you really don't have time to think, your real personality comes out. There are all kinds of personality quizzes, tests, and assessments you can take. You may want to do that, but how about thinking back in your life to when you were faced with adversity. What did you do? Did you retreat? Did you stand up and fight? Did you fall to your knees and cry out for help? Did you blame someone else? Or did you take a deep breath, assess the situation and walk calmly through?

There is not one wrong way of responding. It takes ALL kinds to make the world livable. Imagine if all of us jumped in to save the day? Or all of us sat back and retreated? It takes the bulldozers, the believers, the helpers, the retreaters. Without each one there would be a lopsided tilt, or an absolutely boring place to live.

I can't help but think of Jesus' disciples – all these manly men hanging out with the Son of God – and how different all their personalities were. One night during a storm, they were on a boat. (Hmmm, so I guess if you're not sure what kind of personality you have, you may need to get on a boat). Anyway, it was stormy and some of the disciples were scared. Then they saw it. A man was walking on the water toward the boat.

Ok, let's pause right here. What would you do? Would you be the bulldozer? Would you be the blamer, the believer, the helper, the hider? Some thought they were seeing a ghost. Yep, I'd definitely be calling ghost busters. Then Jesus calls out to them to tell them not to worry.

One of the disciples, Peter (the bulldozer) says, "Lord, if it is you, tell me to come to you on the water." (Matthew 14) In typical take-charge kind of fashion, Peter wanted in on the action, not sure at all what would happen. I am pretty sure Peter had never walked on water before. And sure enough, it was harder than he thought.

Immediately, when he took his eyes off Jesus, he began to sink. Although it doesn't say this in the Bible, I am betting that Peter started going down dramatically, in a panic. He may have even screamed like a girl. But Jesus took a breath and calmly reached out and grabbed his hand and pulled Peter back in the boat as the waves calmed down. I imagine them laughing hysterically. As the adrenalin wore off they cracked up!

Whether you are the bold-in-your-face one, the calm-precise one, the sit-back-and-soak-it-in one, or the let's-pray-and-hold-hands one, you need to own it! God has made you that way – it's part of your signature!

I have learned to calm my crazy-take-charge kind of personality down a bit, but truth is, THAT is who I am. Just the other day during a potluck dinner a lady was choking. There were 80 other people there including an EMT, a police officer and a firefighter. But, of course, I swiftly jumped up and started running to 'save the day', when I realized I probably was not equipped for the task at hand. Yes, you are unique and your personality suits you. Own it and be thankful for it!

Chapter 5

LET'S GO EUROPE

"Make no apologies for your personality." –the goodvibe.com

Maybe I've got you thinking? Are you realizing that you are here, like no one else that has ever walked the earth before, for a reason, and with a purpose? It's not by accident you are reading this at this moment in time! You are you for a reason!

After college graduation, my best friend and I decided to go on a backpacking tour to Europe. Our only source of education was a "Let's Go Europe" book that my friend checked out of the library-before the era of full google search from anywhere. We were so naïve, so young, and well … just plain dumb. We packed our backpacks and planned to see the sights, make the world a better place, and maybe fall in love (that was my hope anyway).

Just to prove how dumb we were, we read in the "Let's Go Europe" book that if we intended to stay in hostels, we should bring our own sheets. So we packed our sheets. Since it said nothing about towels, we didn't pack towels. For weeks, we had to dry off with our bed sheet that took up half of our pack.

We bought a Euro-rail pass so we could jump on the train and go anywhere it would take us! In the handy "Let's Go Europe" book, we learned that young people could stay at youth hostels. They offered very affordable lodging and were scattered all across Europe. There are so many stories from this three-week trip. So many opportunities to grow and learn, but there is one incident that helped me 'find' myself more than any other thing we did (and we did a lot).

Halfway through our trip, we landed a timeshare condo at a resort in St. Johann im Pongau- Salzburg, Austria. After living in stinky, coed hostels, this room was pretty close to heaven! We were able to shower, wear bath robes, dry off with a *towel* and watch TV, even if it was all in Dutch!

Because we were in the Alps, we decided to take advantage of God's beautiful creation and explore! We happened upon the adventure of "canyoning". For those of you non-extreme-sport-people, canyoning is a sport where you swim, rappel and jump down the waterfalls of the Swiss Alps. This particular sport is illegal in the US. That should've been my first clue.

For this adventure we relied on ourselves, a tight-fitting wet suit and a guide who barely spoke English. We were living on the edge now! After the initial shock of the water temperature -I didn't know the rivers and streams are from the snow melting-I was starting to love this exciting adventure. We would swim through the rocks, feet first, making it to a drop off. Sometimes we would simply climb down, and other times we'd have to rappel or jump. The rushing, clear water and beautiful scenery was invigorating to every sense.

Our guide kept using English cuss words to explain how difficult some things would be. (Like I said, he knew "some" English). This dangerous adventure was turning out to be amazing, in all kinds of ways!

After two or three small falls, we came to the first big challenge. We had to rappel down a fall because it was pretty steep, yet it was too shallow to just jump. The guide tied a rope around my waist, used a carabineer to secure me and tried to explain how to back down the rock as he let out the rope. My friend made it down easy. As the water was rushing over the rock, the guide let out the slack of the rope. My feet were stuck on the rock, but the guide didn't know and he continued to let out inches, then feet, of the rope.

I was completely upside down as gallons of water rushed over me. The sound of the water pouring into my brain through my nose was deafening and I could not hear nor see a thing.

I was going to drown. Right there, I was going to meet my Creator, in the Swiss Alps.

Thoughts of my parents flashed through my mind. They would have to ship my body back to America. What an awful phone call that would be. What a stupid, selfish way to die! It seemed like I was there for an hour, (maybe two). I must've blacked out because the next thing I knew my friend was helping me stand in waist-deep water.

The guide bounced down and scolded me, again using a ton of explicit language intermingled with German and Dutch. Not sure what I did wrong, or why he yelled at me, I just knew from then on I would need to be more careful.

At this time in our adventure I had a heightened awareness of my life. Death seemed real, my relationships seemed more meaningful, and I felt like I had to make it home no matter what. After a few more jumps, rappels and climbs, we made it to the grand finale. After jumping off a 15-foot fall, we swam to a tiny rock. (And I mean TINY! My feet hung off every side). Thirty-five feet below, the water slammed into a shallow swirling pool. It was obviously the end of our tour. The only way out was to jump out to the left and swim hard away from the massive falls that could pull you under.

Trust me, I asked my guide at least a hundred times if there was another way. Standing on that slippery, small rock, every single muscle in me was utterly tense. The guide was yelling curses at me, my friend below was bellowing encouraging words and I was trying to give myself the biggest pep talk I had ever heard. I could not go back the way I came – that was certainly impossible – but *how* could I jump, without slipping, hitting the rock, and then swim to safety?

I WAS FROZEN. I couldn't do it. I stood on that rock for three hours. (Ok it really wasn't three hours – maybe 15 minutes – but if felt like forever). I HAD TO JUMP. Why couldn't I jump?

Have you ever been there? Completely and utterly stuck? Your mind is telling you to move, but your body completely refuses. It's the most surreal feeling. Maybe it's happened to you – speaking up in class, entering into that contest, applying for the job – you're on the ledge but can't seem to push through.

I'm not really sure what pushed me in, but something did. Something from WAY down inside literally propelled my body off the rock. I did it. I finally jumped! And it was amazing. (But no, I would never ever do it again and I forbid any of you to try!)

Pulling myself out of that water was the most invigorating thing I had ever done. You know those adrenaline junkies – they do this kind of stuff all the time – and now I know why. Every single nerve in my body was fired up! I bet my hair was even standing on end. I felt so alive, every single fiber in my body had a purpose. Coming that close to death and overcoming truly made an impact on me. My desire was to feel alive like that everyday--without the jumping and almost dying part. I want to have such a sturdy resolve to live that my neurons are fired up and ready to make a difference every single day.

You may still be questioning if you have a purpose. But the deal is, even the core fiber of your being knows you have a purpose. There is a reason you automatically breath or your heart beats. Your body wants to live! You have a reason. Now please please do not go and jump off a cliff to find that purpose! Just take my word for it! YOU are you for a reason!

"Leadership is the art of getting someone else to do something you want done because he wants to do it." – Dwight D. Eisenhower

Finding your Passion in

Leadership

Chapter 6

THAT FOUR LETTER WORD

"Fear—an unpleasant emotion caused by the belief that someone or something is dangerous." Webster Dictionary

That four letter word – FEAR.

It's a four-letter word – at least in my opinion – because it has more power to hurt, tear down, change the course of direction, or completely stop someone dead in their tracks than anything else on Earth. Any way you look at it, fear has way too much power in our lives.

How has fear deterred you from your goal this week, this season or this year? How have you let fear derail you from your path to success? How many times have you changed your mind, your direction or your desire because of fear?

As a coach I hear excuse after excuse of how something is "unattainable" or "can't be done". Every day I hear of a new reason or a new way of labeling fear. We all do it. In our relationships, our work, and our every decision, fear seems to rule.

My three kids have always been scaredy-cats. They're afraid of the dark, the boogie man, of monsters, of getting in trouble! IT WEARS ME OUT! I was raised having no fear, almost to a fault. So when I live with four overly cautious creatures, it's exhausting. Each day is a battle for them to let fear control them or the other way around.

Today I took my daughters to our local amusement park for one last summer fling. It was 100 degrees, an hour away, and ridiculously expensive. But hey, I'm making memories I told myself. My youngest was bound and determined to conquer her fear and ride the roller coaster with two loops.

First, we rode the mini roller coaster, the big ship that rocks you out of control, the water log and even the big dropping ride (that I admittedly hate). It was a great day. The lines were short, and the rides were fun. But we still had not reached the double looped roller coaster that she vowed she would ride.

Abby is my youngest and has always – I mean "straight from the womb" always – been in charge. She calls the shots. She is super strong-willed, yet sensitive enough to make you feel like you are the one who made the decision.

She is tiny for her age and cute as a button. Her long sandy brown hair frames her giant smile with a perfect twinkle in her dark brown eyes. This is the perfect combination for intense leadership. She was voted class president in kindergarten and has not been voted out nor impeached since (according to her). She is accustomed to getting her way.

Although Abby has a strong will and an iron clad leadership quality, she still allows fear to take over. She has only slept by herself about three or four times in the decade she's been alive. It's a given when her brother and sister are not home that she sleeps with us (thanking the Lord we have a king-size bed). She will not get more than 10-20 feet from me when we are out and about, and she won't venture far into something that she is not familiar with.

So this day at the Amusement Park she used her determined will to overcome that fear. It was beautiful to watch her take control and be bigger than her anxiety. She took me by the hand and we got in line for the DOUBLE LOOP roller coaster. I could literally hear the inner discussion going on in her little brain and I saw fear swirling in her eyes. But she overcame! She rode it. She conquered her fear. When asked how she overpowered her fear, she simply said "I was scared, but I just did it! Then I did it again, because it wasn't so bad."

She just did it! Oh how easy that sounds, but oh how profound. Just do it. So many times the fear of rejection, the fear of failure, or the fear of success will freeze us from doing anything. But the answer is JUST DO IT!

Marty, my sweet, amazing husband, has let fear stop him many times from stepping toward his dreams. He is overly cautious and tends to err on the "safe" side. Recently he was asked to audition for a southern gospel quartet. He sings really well, and absolutely loves it. He used to sing in an acappella group when he was younger, was a choir member during high school and college, and has always been part of the praise team at our church. However, the mere idea of "auditioning" caused him anxiety.

He texted me a couple of days before the audition:

"Well, honey, you don't have to ask others about their fears. You have a husband you can write a whole book on regarding fears. Here's my fear ... At first my fear about this was just the thought of doing it! I'm trying to overcome that fear just *by* actually doing it. Now my MAJOR fear about it is trying to do something that I would LOVE to be able to do, yet I'm realizing I'm not REALLY capable of doing it. Not a fear of not making it, but a fear of not being able to actually succeed at it. How do you overcome the fear of failure when it's almost guaranteed?"

Have you ever had that conversation? It is hard to hear that someone is not even trying because they are fearful of not succeeding. They're letting the fear ALREADY dictate the outcome.

One of my friends told me she never learned to drive. At age 44, she has to rely on everyone else – or public transportation – because she has always let fear decide for her. And let me tell you … once you feed that fear, it gets bigger! The longer you give into it, the stronger it gets. At age 16, you may have a little fear of driving, but add three decades of submitting to that fear, and the task will feel nearly impossible.

I remember getting to the end of a high dive at the public swimming pool. Everyone made it look SO easy! Just jump off, right? But fear always seemed to creep in. Funny thing is, the longer I stood there, the bigger the fear became. It was like a wet gremlin or one of those tiny sponges you put into water that grows right before your eyes. The more you dwell on that fear, the stronger and bigger it gets.

Luckily, Marty didn't let his fear derail him. He had a scheduled audition, and he actually HAD to face his fear. As a loving, encouraging wife should, I reassured him, I pumped him up and I prayed for him. In return, he confided, "I told the Lord I don't want to worry or be fearful of this. It's in His hands to do with it as He desires. I'll go do my very best and then hopefully sleep peacefully tonight."

He just did it! And guess what … he did sleep peacefully! AND his fear-conquering muscle just got a little stronger! Yes, he did make it and is now the tenor for X-alt Gospel Quartet. Take that fear.

One of my favorite quotes comes from "philosopher" Will Smith in his movie After Earth. In this film, Smith is guiding his son on a path that will help him overcome any kind of obstacle. He says, "If we are going to survive this, you need to remember, fear is not real. It is a product of the thoughts you create. Now do not misunderstand me – danger is very real. But fear is a choice."

Danger is real, but fear is a choice.

My goal is to help you identify your fear as actual fear and then overcome it by Just Doing It. Have you ever started a project or task and before you know it, had every excuse in the book not to finish? Maybe it was to call your client list, or apply for a job. Maybe you desired to start a conversation, or simply attend a meeting. You came up with every reason not to. It's easy to do and we all fall victim to it.

Once when I was making some follow-up calls, I said out loud "It's noon, so no one is going to answer. I might as well not call." I was totally making an excuse. But was that really why I didn't want to call them? NO WAY! I was choosing fear. Fear they would say no, fear that I would feel like a failure, fear that I would waste my time. Funny thing is, I identified that my excuse was out of fear, and I decided to just do it anyway. And as Abby would say, "It wasn't that bad, so I did it again."

So how about a little challenge? Next time you intend to make an excuse I challenge you to say it out loud. Once you say it out loud, then question it. Have a heart-to-heart conversation with yourself. Be honest. You will find out that it may be coming from a fear.

The next step is to identify that fear. Once you've identified the fear, then you can determine if it is danger or fear you are choosing. You have the power to choose. Remember, fear is optional.

Let's practice. What is something you have put off doing? Joining a church? Making a phone call? Applying for a job? Auditioning? Whatever it is, write it down.

_____

Next, write down why you have not gone further.

_____

Once you have identified the excuse, identify the fear. What is it? Write that down.

_____

Is it so bad? If that potential client says no, or you don't get the job, is that so bad? You may not get the part, you might even make a fool of yourself, but in the grand scheme of things is that so bad?

Life is too short to live in fear. You have the capacity to choose—live in that fear or not? "God has not given us a spirit of fear …" 2 Timothy 1:7

Chapter 7

CONSISTENCY

*"Consistency is better than rare moments
of greatness." -author unknown*

I played basketball. It was something I loved. Since third grade I would dribble a basketball everywhere I went. Every summer I would attend summer camps, and every fall, you'd find me in a gym. The game of basketball was second nature. I loved being on the court. Being a short, clumsy girl, my natural ability had to be overcome by pure determination. I had to work harder and longer to develop skills my teammates possessed naturally.

I would stay after practice in high school every day to shoot 100 three-pointers. I shot so many three-pointers that I developed a bone spur in my right wrist. Even so, I ended up ranking third in the entire state for three-point average!

To add to my excitement, during my freshman year in college I set a school record. In one game I was 10 for 10 at the three-point line! (Coach Story … Remember, I had licorice and bean dip before the game!) After that I was unstoppable. It seemed all those extra hours in the gym paid off! The muscle memory, the accuracy, the form all clicked and I was a force to be reckoned with at the three-point line.

The Compound Effect by Darren Hardy is one of my favorite books. Hardy refers to the "compound effect"[2] as the 8th wonder of the world and I tend to believe him. In his book, Hardy shares that if you consistently do something over a long enough time, it will compound and you will have ULTIMATE results.

For example, eating a small bowl of ice cream at night may not hurt you. In fact, it's a lovely way to end the day. Eat a bowl of ice cream every single day for a year, and all of a sudden you will see a difference! The opposite is also true. Doing a few extra push-ups would not merit that much change. But doing extra push-ups every single day consistently will compound to a great effective chest muscle.

One of my favorite examples Hardy uses is the penny-a-day analogy. If you were given the choice of $3 million cold hard cash, or a penny a day (that doubled in value each day) for only 31 days, which one would you choose?

---

[2] Hardy, Darren <u>The Compound Effect: Jumpstart Your Income, Your Life, Your Success. NY, 2010. 10-11</u>

If you chose the penny a day, you're at a whopping $5.12 on day 10, but if you chose the $3 million, you're still at $3 million! By day 20, you've earned over $5,000 – not bad, but still nowhere near $3 million. However, with the compounding penny, on day 31, you would have $10,737,418.24![3]

The consistent effort over a period of time truly makes a difference.

So let's get a little more practical. If you are like me, you are desperate for a quick fix! Our society has conditioned us to expect instant gratification! We want clear skin NOW, we want instant income NOW, we want everything NOW NOW NOW! The truth is, good things DO come to those who wait!

Let's get personal. How about your eating habits? How many times have you said something like "I'm going to lose 10 pounds by spring break!" or something of the sort? Eating healthy, or eating less for a short period of time, will not give you the desired outcome! It's changing small things every single day for an extended period of time that will help you reach amazing results.

Consistency is the key. Starting a diet every Monday will tear down your desire to reach those goals. The effort it takes to start and stop over and over will deplete your morale! But

---

[3] Hardy, Darren <u>The Compound Effect: Jumpstart Your Income, Your Life, Your Success. NY, 2010. 10-11</u>

making a small change and doing it every day will work. Use the example of the Tortoise and the Hare. The Tortoise just habitually and reliably trekked on. Consistently moving. Not trying to take short cuts, or change perspective, he just trudged on, over and over. The Hare started, then stopped, over and over again. His approach was not consistent, and in the end he lost.

I've heard a story about an expedition including two groups of explorers from two different countries. They were going to journey across rough terrain to stake claim in uncharted territory. As both groups prepared, they charted their plans. One group would hike 20 miles every day no matter what. Rain, shine, freezing conditions or perfect weather, they would trudge exactly 20 miles each day. This feat was later named the 20-mile-march. [4]

The other party was less consistent. Their plan was to go as far as they could and rest when needed. Some days they would reach 40 or 50 miles, other days they were too sore and would rest all day. Every day was different and they trudged on.

Although they had the same distance, the same weather and the same rations, only one group made it, staked their claim, and made it back. Yep, you guessed it, the consistent group triumphed! A little bit every day paid off greatly. Every voyager

---

[4] Collins, Jim. http://www.jimcollins.com/articletopics/articles/how-to-manage-through-chaos.html

in the consistent group made it there and back alive. The other group was not as fortunate. Not only did they never make it to the final destination, but most perished as well.

It pays to do a little often.

There are many things in my life I do consistently. I am super consistent in eating candy. Each and every day, I unfailingly eat candy. The compound effect is headaches, fatigue and tummy issues. Eating candy sporadically and inconsistently may not have had these effects on me.

It is true that if you do something long enough, you'll see astounding effects! I've also been consistently disciplined in journaling. I have volumes of journals. On these pages I have poured out my frustrations, thanksgivings, longings, and joyful moments. I have consistently penned positive quotes and scriptures. I have written stories about my kids, my job, my life.

Through these stacks of journals I have learned so much about my family, myself, and my Creator. Each day I jotted down my thoughts, and now as I'm writing this book, I discovered I have droves of material! They are like history volumes that I can pour through and share with others. What a joy!

Whatever your desired result, I challenge you to do something toward that goal each and every day for six solid months!

You may consider that a crazy long time, but you are worth it! Create a chart or grid and affix happy faces or star stickers every time you do it! Eventually you will start to see change. Maybe not the 10th day, 2nd month or even ¾ of the way there, but toward the end of these months, I guarantee you'll see a great change!

Maybe your goal is to compliment your spouse every single day, say a true prayer of thanksgiving, park a mile from work, take the stairs instead, eat a salad instead of a hamburger, call a client each and every day, or stop eating after 7:00 pm. Whatever it is – BE CONSISTENT! And please share the compound effects once you receive them!

Chapter 8

SERVANT LEADERSHIP

"It is amazing what you can accomplish when you do not care who gets the credit." -Harry S. Truman

If you have ever read books about leadership or heard speakers talk about leadership, it is highly likely you've heard the term "servant leadership". In most aspects this seems to be an oxymoron. One may think leadership is from the front like a drum major waving his baton leading his band. To think of a leader becoming less than or "below" the ones he leads feels wrong somehow. The truth is, however, that true leaders are those who are selfless and want more for the people they lead than they do for themselves.

One of my favorite experts on leadership teaches and talks a lot about servant leadership. John Maxwell has written numerous books on this topic and many of his amazing quotes come to mind. To save time and energy, I'll just quote one or two and hope you buy one of his best selling books!

In one of my favorite Maxwell quotes, he says "When you become a leader, you give up your right to think about yourself first. Leadership is always about others first."[5]

Clearly, Maxwell's definition of leadership is PUTTING OTHERS FIRST! It's all about becoming less so your team, your organization, your congregation, your family or whoever you are leading becomes more.

When I graduated college I was offered my dream job coaching women's basketball at the college level. So what if the college was a tiny Bible College, and so what if it had never had a women's basketball team. I was going to be the pioneer women's basketball of that college and bring it! The summer before moving down I prayed, I planned, and I organized my entire strategy. I pondered on what drills to practice, what plays to run, what to do on road trips – it was my dream come true.

I was to report to the college for staff/faculty meetings August 15. Students started moving on campus August 22. The first day on the job I was called into the Dean of Student's office. Feeling very small and insignificant, I was informed that the Athletic Director (who also coached men's basketball) was no longer on staff. Okay, so this is a weird start to my dream job, I thought, but I had learned to become flexible. The next thing

---

[5] Maxwell, John. <u>The 21 Irrefutable Laws of Leadership: Follow Them and People Will Follow You</u>. Nashville, TN 2007

he wanted to share with me was completely unexpected – "We want to offer you the position of Athletic Director!"

Say what?

Excuse me, you want a 22-year-old woman – ok, really a girl – with zero college coaching experience, to run an entire athletic department?! Of course I will! If you keep my personality in mind, you are probably not surprised. Looking back now, I see how naïve I was! I had no clue what it meant to be A.D.! I had to fire, hire, schedule, balance a budget, run concessions, pick uniforms, maintain all the athletic equipment, supplies, building and fields, clean and wax floors – and all this on top of coaching my precious team.

I was the Athletic Director! I was "big coach on campus" now! So let's meet my team!

Three girls came to the women's basketball meeting the first week of school. THREE?! It takes five to play, and we need at least 2-3 subs on the bench. The A.D. before me did a great job scheduling games, but failed to get players. We had a 31-game schedule against some GIANT teams, and I only had three players. This was going to be an interesting year.

Walking the halls of the girl's dorm I asked if anyone, ANYONE played basketball, or could run? It was pitiful. I had girls come out that had never – and I mean never – picked up a basketball.

I was getting worried. Our first scrimmage against a huge Division-I school was the tell-tale sign that this year was going to be the worst year of my career.

One of the dorm recruits was to pass the ball in bounds after the other team's made basket. Rules state that after a shot is made the opposing team takes the ball out of bounds, then passes in bounds to a player. My newbie took the ball out of bounds and then started dribbling down court. Perfectly ok if you are playing peewee league. BUT NOT COLLEGE BALL. The poor referee did not know what to do. He looked at me, looked at her and blew the whistle. Other team's ball. Turnover. This stuff happened the entire year.

It's no lie that we lost every game by an average of 100 points. Game in and game out I would cringe as the other team lit up the score board and my team came to the locker room with heads held low and sometimes tears on their cheeks.

It was a very long year.

During one game, the opposing coach came over to the bench – in the middle of the game – to apologize. To say the least, it was humbling.

I remember thinking I never ever want to put my team, my girls or myself in that kind of situation again, so I took action. One thing about these horribly humbling experiences – it causes action. As leader, coach, "mama-bear" to these girls who were just helping me out, I wanted to protect them. When you are knocked out every single game, it is daunting and exhausting. You can beat me every day, but when you hurt my team my reaction was "Oh no you didn't!" It was my job as their leader to step in and make a change. I had to do the work and serve them.

Every week, after every loss, we would search scripture to find meaning. We tried to find the good out of these losses, the beauty in the ashes. We would pray, cry, lament. We became super close and our team learned to identify with a Savior who was beaten and experienced much loss. Although I learned so much about myself, how to lead and how to serve, I never wanted to put a team through that again.

It is easy to spot a superficial leader. Those who want the accolades or the money only will fizzle out. The ones who WANT the best for those they lead are the real deal. A great litmus test for you when you are considering leading is this question:

WHO AM I DOING THIS FOR?

Of course you want to reach your own personal goals and achieve greatness, but if that is the only "who" in your equation, you will not be successful.

Another famous quote this time by Zig Ziglar says it best: "If you help enough people get what they want, you'll end up getting what you want."[6]

As I dreamed of becoming a coach I never realized the people in my circle would have an impact in my journey. I forgot to consider those individuals who called me coach! I was already dusting my trophies before I realized the true meaning of leading a team. The responsibility for their well being was on me. It wasn't just me losing, it wasn't just me hurting and being humbled – it was these treasured seven girls who showed up day in and day out, only to feel their spirits plummet. It clicked. It is not all about me. When I serve them, we ALL grow.

Maybe you have had a teacher or coach like that, someone who would stay up past bedtime and go out of her way to push you to be successful. Maybe it was a parent. How many times has your mom forfeited the last swig of milk, or the last donut? How many times did she come pick you up at midnight when she'd rather be snug in bed? We all know someone who has displayed true servant leadership. They handle the behind the scenes "get no glory" kind of acts and it always highlights their servant leadership.

---

[6] Economy, Peter. "21 Zig Ziglar Quotes to Inspire Your Success in Life and Business." Inc.com. Icons of Entrepreneurship, 2 Oct. 2015. Web. 3 Nov. 2016.

In first grade my daughters had a reading challenge. They had to read all year long to hit a goal and when they made it they could participate in this great big celebration. It was the "ball" of first grade and every one strived to achieve this great accomplishment. This task was difficult for savvy readers and almost impossible for struggling ones. So when my daughter's classmate, "Johnny", worked extra hard people took notice. My daughter came home exclaiming over how many books "Johnny" had read! "Mom, he works harder than ever!" She was noticing.

The party came and "Johnny" woke up with a fever. It was totally devastating for him and I know it completely broke his heart. Even his classmates at the party felt the void of this hard worker – especially his teacher. Mrs. McCoy is a servant leader. She comes early, stays late and never complains. She loves those students like they were her own and truly wants to see them succeed.

Although Mrs. McCoy has three kids and a busy schedule herself, she gathered snacks, mementos and party favors and at 3:45 pm drove to "Johnny's" house. She brought the party to HIM! Balloons, streamers and celebration came knocking at his front door.

The only way others knew about this gesture is when he returned to school the next day. Grinning from ear to ear, he shared how much Mrs. McCoy loved him and wanted him to be a "super reader"!

It's important to stay observant because stories like that happen all the time. Visiting "Johnny" after school hours will NOT give her a raise or bonus, it will not make him smarter, but it will show the students Mrs. McCoy leads that she cares more about them than she does for herself. WOW, I want to serve like that!

It is impossible to talk about servant leadership without mentioning Jesus. As the son of God, He came to this sinful world not only to share God's love, but to demonstrate a sacrificial kind of love. He even said, "I did not come to be served but to serve." The fact that the man who made the Heavens and Earth wanted to heal the sick, fix hearts or cry with the wounded blows my mind! He didn't come demanding a crown or mansion, nor an endorsement – he simply came to serve.

Are you a servant leader? Are your motives to promote those under you or lift yourself? Consider it closely. Although this world teaches us to lead from the front, true leadership comes through leading from behind.

Chapter 9

HUMILITY – EEK!

"It is not thinking less of yourself, but thinking of your self less." –Dreaming in 3D by Doug Clay

I've always been a competitive person. I'm not sure if it's learned or taught, but in any and all activities, I want to be at the top. I want to win. I want the prize.

The first big fight Marty and I had was over an UNO game. As he laid down his second to last card, I yelled "UNO" before he could. That's when it hit the fan. "You have to give me a chance," he pled.

No I don't.

Sometimes passion and competitiveness is not a good combination. After 16 years, I'm not sure we've ever settled that argument, but we have learned to never play against one another again.

(Lesson here loved ones—life it too short. We are on the same team. Let your sweet competitive loved one win gracefully and don't be a sore loser).

Being in sales, a competitive drive to reach the top will help. Not only did I want that big fat commission, but the recognition was the kicker! In Chris Brady's book *Launching a Leadership Revolution*, he states that there are three levels to leading.[7]

The first, and most obvious level, is money. Making money gets you in. Leaders see the financial benefit and will go for it. Once you get that first fat paycheck, you're hooked – level one, check! If a leader stays at this level, eventual burn out is inevitable. There is only so much money can buy and no matter how much you have –it'll never be enough.

The second tier of leadership is recognition. This is stronger than the pull of money. And I believe that. For so long I was a self-hater and when I started to hear good things about myself through my successful sales, it became a drug. I needed more. I wanted more. I loved seeing my name on the top, I loved hearing my name called out, I loved the accolades, the titles, the "air-brushed" pictures. Beware the cliché is right on—it is lonely at the top—and may I add--stressful and exhausting.

---

[7] Brady, Chris, and Orin Woodward. Launching a Leadership Revolution. NYC: Business Plus Hatchet Group, 2005. Print.

The last level that will keep a leader going according to Woodward is life destiny—fulfilling your purpose here on Earth. When a leader gets to this level, money and accolades mean nothing unless you are making a difference by doing what you were put on Earth to do. Few leaders get here and most stay on the eternal hamster wheel for more money and more recognition, however some do rise to their life destiny level. I finally feel like I've arrived here at level three, but it was a humbling journey.

I was stuck in level two for a long time. I chased the next incentive, sometimes at all costs. I put family, church, and self on the back burner to get to that next promotion. It is and was extremely exhausting! I would arrive and was never satisfied. I would work my tail off to sometimes fall short and be blind to the benefits of what I had accomplished.

Being at the top was the only motivator. Unfortunately, it was all about me, and how I would feel. Regrettably, one of my quotes on stage was "I just love seeing my name in lights!" Can you imagine? Sometimes the rewards were amazing and I reveled in them, but other times I would brush it aside to move to the next.

Not worth it.

I can see how people stuck in this cycle become workaholics. It's never ending, and "much" is never enough. Although I was at the top of my game, I needed the next incentive to give me the rush. The addiction to the "lights" truly blinded me to who I was leading and how I was leading them. Finding my worth in a title was fleeting and I did learn the fall from the top is painful.

When you are using pride and acknowledgment as the primary motivation to do your job, God will not honor it. In fact, a Bible verse I learned as a tot was "Pride comes before the fall". And yes, my friends, it does. At the top of my game, top in the company, with a title only 22 of us out of 100,000 plus women attained, I had arrived. Although my team, my family and my "followers" wanted to be where I was, I knew the true motivation was not going to sustain me.

Then it happened. Company structure changed and I had to demote myself. I had 18 months to hit certain numbers, which would be possible, but it would take me working 24/7, ignoring my family, and throwing myself into work. God and I came face to face, and through a conversation with the CEO, He spoke right to my soul. Through her, He said, "Heidi, if you are trying to stay at the top because of your pride, then God will never ever bless your business." Ouch. What a slap in the face.

Along came embarrassment, shame, fear, doubt ... in my mind it would've been easier to be hit by a bus or struck by some Ebola plague. I had to face the people I had trained, poured into, encouraged and tell them I felt like a failure! It's harder than you think. Oh how I'd like to be anywhere else, I realized.

Remember Jesus talking to the rich young ruler? The ruler truly loved Jesus. He said so. He even asked how he could serve and love Jesus more. Jesus knew the ruler was proud, He knew the ruler enjoyed the tributes, the honors, the position. When asked to go sell all that he owned and humbly follow, the rich young ruler was unable to lay his pride down. I know exactly how he felt. He could see the headlines "Rich Young Ruler Loses Everything to Follow Homeless Guy." He had a reputation and it was more important than his relationship with Christ.

Let me caution you. I am a sinner and I struggle daily with my arrogance. I know that I put on an air so that others will look and think "I want to be like Heidi." I struggle, yes. However, I have learned that people in my life have responded and have come to life more when I am vulnerable, broken and not at the top of my game. They can relate and want to be exposed, too, so they do not have to keep chasing the next carrot dangling.

It's true – beloved, raw-real-truth is utterly more attractive than an "I've got it all" façade. Try it. Get with a close friend and share your heart. God is asking you to lay it down so He can use you!

I'm not saying it won't hurt – it will – but it is entirely and downright worth it.

I recently visited a good friend in the hospital. Linda is battling Crohn's disease, and this past year it has knocked her down quite a bit. She has fought for her life and is enduring constant pain. Linda is a diva, always adorably dressed in the newest and latest fashion. She has cute nails, perfectly matched jewelry, and a smile that will warm your soul.

Lying in a hospital bed in a paper thin gown can really overshadow said trendiness. However, one thing I noticed with Linda is that I didn't even notice! As she shared with me her struggles, all I saw was beauty! It wasn't until I wanted to take a selfie of us that she mentioned how ugly she must look! She was completely and utterly beautiful to me, because I knew her heart. We took the selfie, and because she is not vain, she posted it on social media!

That is how I want to be! No need to worry about the outside – it's enough to know I'm pretty on the inside.

So where are you, my friend? What is driving you in your current leadership position? Do you want more or would you be willing to lose it all so that you can be real? Maybe you have arrived at a comfortable level. Maybe you know the limits of your motivation or perhaps you've been inspired to jump off the vicious cycle. Whatever the case, know that your purpose as a leader is far more than a paycheck or position – it's about the people that follow you.

Chapter 10

GOAL SETTING

"Setting a goal is not the main thing. It is deciding how you will go about achieving it and staying with the plan." -Tom Landry

No matter whether they are hard goals, smart goals, big goals or bite size goals, write your goals down, make your goals a mantra, visualize your goals, post your goals in color, make a goal board, yada yada!

You're probably saying to yourself, "Oh my word we get it! Set goals already!"

Someone who has been in leadership her entire life realizes that goal setting is common practice. Funny thing is, it seems to become more and more forced or rehearsed. Like that trite Sunday School answer, we tend to fill in the blanks of what we should be wanting to shoot for. Looking back, I've noticed my goals were not heartfelt and actually pretty lame sometimes. But however ridiculous my goals have been, it does not diminish the journey one bit.

Goals always seemed to be part of our household, especially when it came to adventure and my sister. We lived on a rolling hill that backed up to a creek. My sister and I would spend hours exploring, climbing trees and getting dirty. My dad tied a ski rope to the highest branch in the yard and we would swing 30-40 feet over the creek. Needless to say, we have many memories, but one stands out above all the others.

Our Hole to China.

Daddy had every "man toy" available. Tractors, back hoes, splitters – you name it – he could tear down things and build it back in one week flat. It was my big-tool-diggin'-daddy that gave us an idea to start digging a hole and see if we could make it to China!

What a goal!

We dreamed of it. What would we see? What animals would we run into? How would gravity pull us in the center of the Earth? What colors of Earth's layers would each step bring? The excitement of that goal was riveting.

Our Goal: China
Our plan: Dig!

And as a 2nd and 4th grader, that seemed enough!

My father used a giant, grey tractor tire to outline the area. Tammy and I started right away. With our little shovels pushing, poking and moving dirt for hours, we still barely made a dent. I remember thinking for a short moment that our goal may be a little too lofty, however, I never mentioned it to my sister! I just kept digging and sweating and digging some more. I was a believer, yet becoming weary.

Then my dad comes over the hill growling and bumping in a big green bouncing tractor with a massive screw-like contraption on the front. As he motions us out of his way, he puts that enormous tool in the earth and it starts spinning. Our hero once again, Dad jutted, bounced and pushed that tool into the earth. With dirt flying to every side, we stood wide eyed and eager to meet our first Chinaman.

After a half day of burrowing, it was finally our turn to finish the dig. We ran as fast as we could to the edge of the gray round tire, just knowing we would see light or perhaps the dark sky on the other side of the planet. We could hardly wait to jump in and fall into China.

It was dark, dingy and smelled like dirt, but we didn't see Chinamen looking back at us, nor the moon shining on the other end of the hole. All we saw was dirt. Cold, smelly dirt.

But it was OK!

Dad threw a rope down and we climbed in and set up shop! It was big enough to hold four kids and we hung "pictures," dug out shelves and played every day from sun up to sun down in our HOLE! Although our goal was China, we were redirected and enjoying every minute! The process to reaching our goal was everything we couldn't even imagine for ourselves. The means to the end became our end after all and we still talk about that hole to China.

If you are spirited enough to set a goal that is unattainable, you may be courageous enough to totally find joy in that journey. You know the old adage: "Shoot for the stars and you may land on the moon." That is so true! What if your goal was to be a *multi*-millionaire and you only landed on millionaire? Imagine if your goal was to bring fresh water to every third world country in the world, yet you *only* supplied 10 or 20 villages!

So maybe it's okay to set crazy, not fully thought out goals. Maybe it's ok to aim for something seemingly out of reach. It really isn't the end goal we remember the most, it's the journey. Like any good road trip, there is a destination in mind, but the stops along the way is what makes it unforgettable.

My daughter plays volleyball. And as in most sports, along with playing volleyball comes a stigma—she must be tall. The truth is, on most select club teams there is a height requirement! So telling a 5'6" fifteen-year-old she's too short to make the team can and does crush dreams. Why would anyone set a goal to play competitive volleyball if you are short?

Why not?

I met a freshman volleyball player from University of Arkansas on a full ride scholarship to play the sport she loved. Coaches all her life dismissed her dream to play at the college level and teams overlooked her because of her height, but her goal was still set! This 5'1" back row defensive specialist had a goal and she worked toward it.

When I asked her why she kept on going after hearing discouragement over and over, her answer was simple, "I loved the game and I wanted to be on the court all. the. time." She knew that the journey working toward that goal would outweigh the end result. In fact, she also told me, "Even if I never got to play college ball, I played every game like I would ONE DAY be there. That's what mattered to me and my coaches."

What are your goals? What have your goals been? Give yourself a check up and assess if you ever HAD goals! Recall the ones you never reached. Were you disappointed? Did you give up on life? Or had you learned something valuable along the way? Maybe you're still reaching and striving for that end result.

Whatever the case, stop and smell the roses! You are actually learning something right now, while you press on toward that giant pie in the sky.

Do not forget to enjoy your journey along the way!

Chapter 11

"FAKE IT 'TIL YOU MAKE IT!"

"Unless we take that first step into the unknown, we will never know our own potential." -Allan Rufus

Sometimes when you are leading, "faking it" is the only thing you can do because the alternative is to not lead at all. I heard a sermon once about Joshua. He was among the group in the Bible that God led out of bondage. Remember, Egypt held all Hebrews as slaves and God used Moses to deliver them out of slavery. Great story with plagues, amazing things and stubbornness.

Although miracle after miracle occurred, the Israelites where obstinate and decided not to obey. Instead of bringing them to the coveted promise land, they had to wander around aimlessly in the wilderness for 40 years! That's a long time to be grounded – my kids should never complain about one week. Crazy, right?!

Finally, after these 40 years, Moses died and Joshua was now the one in charge, the big man on campus, boss-man, leader. God told Joshua to lead the people over the Jordan river into the Promise Land.

What?!

"God, excuse me, um, you see, I am just a wanderer. I know how to wander, I've been wandering for 40 years, since a little tot. In other words, I'm an expert wanderer. Not sure I can lead anyone to the Promise Land." I'm sure Joshua thought of every single excuse he could. Feeling ill-equipped and very vulnerable, Joshua had to fake it until he could make it. Joshua knew his people were tired of drifting – they were desperate to put some roots down, build a house, plant a garden. He was the one who had to guide them into what they really wanted. Instead of giving into his fear and inadequacy, he took one step at a time, with confidence, and his people followed him.

As leaders sometimes we have to do the same! We may not know what lies beyond the horizon or around the corner, but your people are looking to you for guidance and direction. Sometimes we have to trick our unbelief into confidence, our inabilities into certainty, and our worry into faith.

Now, hear me out ya'll, do not lead a group of student doctors into surgery and tell them to fake it until we make it! The principle I'm referring to is basic confidence in ourselves. Yes, you may have no idea if your company will turn it around financially, but you can have confidence that you will and can take one step at a time leading your employees to victory. You may not know if your team will win, or your family will respond, but you can act like they will. BELIEVE, and trick your mind and actions into living it out.

Many memories of confident people swirl in my mind. My Dad, Grandpa(s) and Uncle(s) seem to always be my heroes. They constantly had a tool, remedy or answer for any problem we faced. My uncle Terry could fix anything, from homemade pancakes – oh glory! – to a 200-ton air conditioning unit. My Papa could get anyone to ski behind his boat and always found the best bargain around. My other Pa built baby beds, made delicious peanut brittle and even now, at age 87, quilts with my beloved Grandy! Confidence oozed around me, and for a long time I thought it was because they just simply knew stuff.

Truth is, they didn't really. Every single skill they learned had a starting point. Each ability mastered started out at the "apprentice" level. Leaders have to take a step into the unknown territory, like it or not. This is called choice. Trailblazers are set apart from ordinary folk because they overcome their doubt and choose to trust anyway. Silly fear creeping up again. But by now, you have the tools to squash it like a bug.

As stated before, I grew up on water. Most of the summer you would find my sister and me in swimming suits. Once my own family grew I knew I wanted to teach my kids to play in water as well. I wanted their sun-kissed faces bouncing around in the boat with their little heads bobbing up and down on the lifejackets. My dream was to have family barbeques and water volleyball in the back yard. So I chose. I didn't let fear stop me from buying a boat or putting in a pool! I didn't let anxiety prevent me from backing up a trailer (although I had never done that) or putting a huge down payment on an in ground pool.

Ya'll, backing up a trailer into a lake on a boat ramp is hard. I MEAN HARD. But it had to be done. I had never done it, but chose to overcome my fear. To go left you need to turn right, but not too much or you jack knife (yes, that's a common term we use while backing up a trailer). Everything is backwards and it took me a very long time to learn to do it. But my friends, my kids and all the onlookers were counting on me to get that boat in the water.

My lack of skill, anxious shaking, and sweaty brow did not discourage my determination. I was all in the "fake it until I make it" mode. One hour and 15 minutes later, we were in the water and ready to ride the waves! My dad had made it look unbelievably easy (but he probably didn't his very first time out). Every time I have to back up the trailer, a slight panic comes over me, especially when there are a lot of onlookers, but I put that truck in reverse with confidence and I fake it until my fear is squashed and making it kicks in.

Maybe there is something you would try if only you could convince yourself to just make an attempt. Start small. Go ahead and invite your in-laws over and make that new recipe you've been wanting to try. Turn on some loud French music, put on your apron and own that kitchen! Crack open that laptop and start a spreadsheet. Give yourself a time frame to figure out that application you've been avoiding. Become the I.T. guru you know is in you. Or how about that art project you've wanted to try or that Zumba class? Get in there and do it. Fake it until you make it!

No one is an expert the first time they try, and for most, neither are they on the 2nd, 5th or 10th try. But don't let that stop you from trying! A friend at church asked me if there is anything I can't do. I think she meant it as a compliment, but I said "nope," and you can do it too!

I am not an expert in drawing and painting, but I love to do it, so I made use of that passion and have actually published a coloring book! I am not a super smart business owner, but I need to make money, so I invest and do it anyway. It's the same thing for everything else in my life – whether it's parenting, singing or working out, I can do them all because I just do, not because I'm an expert and have been trained! I fake it and pull it off.

Joshua just made one step and then another. His people were watching, and had no idea what was going on in his head.

All they saw was confidence and determination. As he was faking it to trick his own mind, his followers were believing and developing an assurance in him as well. Sometimes (okay, most of the time) the leader may not know the answers or what tool to use, but he is still the leader and he is willing to try. A leader may be shaking in his boots, but a leader still must lead.

Chapter 12

BROKEN RECORDS

"Be careful of how you are talking to yourself because you are listening." -Lisa M. Hayes

Our brain is an amazing organism. I just cannot believe how intricate and complex it is. The neurons fire from synapses to the other like electricity and sight, smell, touch, taste and things heard are all processed and filed into millions of different places. Memories are stored, words are recorded and visions are like syndicated reruns. There is nothing concrete about these elements, but somehow they are 100% REAL. And it blows my mind – pun intended.

That got me thinking. How can the brain differentiate between *memories* of words and actual live conversation? Or how can the brain tell the difference between the *memory* of a sour pickle or the *actual* bite of a pickle? And what about words? Can the brain know the distinction between actual valid words spoken and words we make up?

I am no expert on the brain – although I did teach one unit on the nervous system to my 5th grader – but my guess is that the brain cannot tell the difference between reality and fantasy. Apart from senses that bring the memory to life, the actual thought of that element cannot be differentiated. Our logic is definitely processed somehow in that tissue, however, we must experience discernment before we act physically.

If someone yells "FIRE" your brain will respond based on the conditioned response. You physically may run, call 911, or yell for help. If someone yells "FIRE" every day for a week, our physical response changes. In one of the flaps in our crazy wrinkled brain, somehow we learn to discern. Or do we?

For years I was a self talker. Not the irrational "I hear voices" kind of talking, but the ashamed, tear myself down kind of talk. Over and over I would tell myself that I'm fat, a horrible mother, unworthy etc. It was a broken record and I was literally brainwashing myself. The memories in my mind from past bad experiences came together in a self-loathing song I would sing every time I messed up or was disappointed in myself.

After consistently singing this badgering song over and over, my physical response kicked in. Remember, my theory is the brain does not always know fact from fiction, and we have conditioned physical reactions to what is played in our minds.

My song went something like this:

"Why did you eat that? You fat stupid idiot, you might as well just give up!"

"You're too stupid to teach your kids, you don't even have enough discipline for yourself."

"Your kids are better off without you. Someone else – anyone else – would lead and teach them better."

Ashamedly, I type those words and remember how natural those thoughts seemed to me at the time. Almost like an old, comfortable couch that really needs to be thrown out. Gag! Telling myself these horrible lies over and over caused a lack of physical discernment. My brained acted as if they were all true! My reaction was to be a bad mom, act with no discipline, and daily contemplate suicide. The broken record played in my brain was causing a physical response that was NOT healthy. This caused me to sing negative messages to myself louder and longer.

What a vicious cycle.

The time, date, or place cannot be dictated, but one day I had had enough. Someone taught me what God my Creator said about me—things like "You are loved, you are worthy, I knew you before you were formed, you are fearfully and wonderfully made, there is no condemnation." I remember these messages from various scriptures, and it was conflicting with the song I wrote and sang myself.

My brain was in conflict and my physical well-being was at stake. My life was on the line, and literally WORDS were going to lead to my death or save me!

Through my sweet husband, loving friends, family, and even my kids, my brain was hearing clashing arguments. One was saying I am precious, I am enough, I am loved, while my personal song blared the opposite. It came down to what was louder. I had to choose what volume the dial would be set on. I had to start conditioning my brain so my physical response was positive.

It was war, and the battle was on. At a leadership conference I actually learned what a mantra was:

man·tra

'mantrə/

noun

noun: mantra; plural noun: mantras

1 (originally in Hinduism and Buddhism) a word or sound repeated to aid concentration in meditation.

◦ a Vedic hymn.

2 a statement or slogan repeated frequently

Traditional religion taught it to change your ways. Say certain things over and over until you have been transformed or renewed. I guess they had my same theory.

As I recovered from shoulder surgery there was a minor set back where my brain signals were not converting to a physical response. In other words, my muscles forgot what to do when my brain told them to. During therapy I was told to talk to my muscles. Yep, I was the crazy lady that would say out loud things like, "Come on bicep pull up my arm." Or "Reach up to wave to that person, now higher, higher."

My physical therapists had me re-conditioning my PHYSICAL response to the words that came out of my mouth! Assuredly, if I would say, "can't, don't, won't" then that would be true! My therapist even told me early on that your body will do what you say. If you say you "can't" then your body believes you! Are you a believer yet? I know it sounds hokey – but please hang with me.

Basically I was "mantra-ing" myself for years! I was concentrating on my negative mantra and letting it literally brainwash me! A new mantra had to take its place.

At the conference I learned about mantras, I literally wrote down a statement of WHO I physically wanted to be. My new mantra included how I wanted to treat my family, what I ate, how I loved and what I did to find joy. The challenge was to read this mantra everyday, out loud.

Honestly, I can say it changed me. At first the transformation was minimum, but was definitely happening. As time went on, the joy that filled my heart was overwhelming. Here's an entry from one of my blogs:

> So, I'm being very vulnerable here! I wrote a mantra back in 2012 and read it almost daily! It went like this:

> *"It's January 2013 and I have 20 or more leaders on my team and I am in the top team sales every month. I eat healthy and inspire others to do so. My kids love and respect me because I am patient and loving with them. I adore my husband and have an awesome intimate relationship with him. I am financially secure and totally blessing others. Others KNOW the love of God because I show them with my life!"*

Maybe you should try!

But where to start right? How about let's start with tradition.

One of my favorite sacred traditional writings is the Bible. Regardless of what you believe, there are some great words of wisdom and it's a great place to begin writing a personal mantra to better oneself. In the book of Romans, the author is writing a letter to a group of believers teaching them how to live their lives. He writes:

"Do not conform to the pattern of this world, but be transformed by the renewing of your mind. Then you will be able to test and approve what God's will is – His good, pleasing and perfect will." Romans 12

So even ancient words teach renewing your mind! So let's start there. My goal was to get rid of my old self and put on my new self!

Let's write your mantra.

Are you ready to change your brain? Simply answer these questions based on WHO and WHAT you are <u>one year from now</u>.

You may want to use a different sheet of paper:

On _____ (date one year from now)

I will

_____

(write exactly how you feel physically, ie. *I will be strong, and healthy. I will eat right. I will be loving and kind to those around me.*)

83

My business/home

_____

_____

_____

(describe your ideal business, your job/ home etc, ie. *I am a hard worker and those around me notice. My home is neat and tidy and I do not complain. My boss notices my hard work. I work with morale and virtue.*)

People around me

_____

_____

_____

_____

(describe the influence you will have on those around you. ie. *I am a servant. I love unconditionally because I care about them. My kids notice. I respond with love and not anger. I am kind, respectful and soft spoken*)

Last step- take all these statements and rewrite them into your mantra, your song! Write it as if you are already that person. Use statements like "I am ... I work ... I share ... I love ..."

Seriously, stop right now and do it.

Congratulations! You have made the first step in training that amazing brain of yours so that you will physically respond in a much healthier and happier manner! Great job.

(Now read this next part out loud)

Great job! I did it! I am on the road to
becoming the person I want to be!
I am capable of doing anything I set my mind to!
I am strong,
I am an overcomer,
I am a new me.

Finding your passionate purpose in

Love

--it's all about relationships—true story

Chapter 13

LOVE LANGUAGE

*"Love is a verb. Without action it is merely
a word." --author unknown*

In January 2013 my sister became a mom for the first time
to three amazing teenagers. And it would prove to be quite
a journey – these children just happen to be from Ukraine.
After a two-year spiritual, emotional, and financial battle to
legally call them their own, I boarded a plane and flew across
the ocean.

My sister and brother-in-law were serving as missionaries
when God finally made them parents. Of course Auntie Heidi
had to meet her niece and two nephews! Although they were
going to come to America just two short months later, I
wanted to meet them in their culture, with their language
and food and all the unique things I would come to love about
them. If my sister gave birth to them, of course I would be in
the hospital room, so why not meet them in their homeland?

After all, that is where the birth of a new family would be taking place.

My flight got in really late, and my niece and nephews were not there to greet me at the airport, much to my disappointment. My sister had waited 13 years for these babies, she was going to start them on a great sleeping schedule (although they were 14, 15 and 16 years old!). So they were not on hand for introductions at such a late hour.

When we got to their house, she told me I could go upstairs and hug them. The minute I opened the bedroom door, this angel sat straight up and even in the dark I could see her perfectly-white beaming smile. IT WAS IMMEDIATE LOVE. I cannot describe it. My heart literally leapt out of my chest and I knew I was the aunt who would cry with her when that boy broke her heart, who would eat chocolate and watch movies, take her shopping and buy her anything she wanted. It was indescribable.

She wrapped her arms around me and said in a very thick Russian accent "Good Morning," though she really meant "Good Night." I was immediately smitten. And that exact scenario happened twice more with my two nephews.

My sister and brother-in-law had been on a team to translate the Bible in the Tatar language. Tatars live among the Ukrainians, but they have always been ostracized. A group considered to be "less than" others, they are outcast and overlooked. My sister has always had a heart for people in such situations so it was no surprise when she was called to assist in translating God's Word for them.

While serving, she also worked at an orphanage where she met Dima and Victor. She volunteered in their first grade class, taking them on field trips, providing gifts and educational material, leading workshops, and spiritually pouring into these institutionalized kids without parents.

She fell in love with each and every child. Dima was the golden child – the bright one, the favored one, the teacher's pet. Victor was not. He was picked on, beaten up, and a little awkward. My sister loved each and every one of the children, but these two had a special place in her heart.

After years of battling infertility, I asked why she would not just adopt. I thought it was as simple as going to the orphanage, picking a kid and then coming home to live Happily Ever After (oh so naïve!). Her words in response pierced me right in my heart—

"How do I pick just one?! How unfair would that be!"

But I knew she wanted to be a real mommy to these kids. She was weary of leaving each day, not knowing what happens at night or when they were sick. She worried that they would not even be taken care of. Her heart was longing but how in the world could she choose?

After much prayer, one child after another was adopted from that class, completely a miracle in itself. Kids in that "special" institution usually don't get adopted – especially almost an entire class – so God was clearly parting the waters. And guess who was standing right there in the middle? --Dima and Victor. The children she was meant to have.

All these years later I still cry tears of joy.

During the entire process of major ups and downs, victories and losses-- I highly recommend you read her blog[8]--she could be writing a book also. She and Matt found that Victor and Dima had sisters and brothers. In Ukraine it was understood that siblings stay together if at all possible. So without hesitation they revised the paper work to verify their willingness to accept not just two kids, but five!

Through the investigation process they discovered that this would actually not be feasible – as it turned out, one brother was too old and one sister was already with a foster family somehow … and then there was Tanya. Our bright-eyed-giant-smiled-curly-red-headed precious Tanya!

Apparently Tanya was truly a "Little Orphan Annie." She is confident, in charge, and mothered everyone in that orphanage. In her eyes, she did not need a family and she was apprehensive

---

[8] grinn.org

at first. Somehow though, my sister wooed her into our family and we cannot imagine life without her.

The first morning when I finally got to spend time with them, Tammy let me share a devotion and she translated. I so badly wanted to talk and ask questions and get to know my niece and nephews, but the language barrier discouraged that. So I tried to act out everything.

Each evening that week I would lie in bed with Tanya and read children's stories in English and try to act out the story. She would laugh until she fell out of the bed. We fell in love. With hardly any words exchanged she, Victor, Dima and I bonded. I WAS THEIR AUNT HEIDI! And we didn't have to say a word — we all just knew it.

I hear all the time how hard it is for some people to believe in God because they can't literally hear Him. They pray and talk but receive no response. I get that. Although communication was a challenge the week I met my new niece and nephews — we probably shared only three or four understandable words the entire time — it did not deter love from growing. We couldn't understand one another and it didn't stop a bond from cultivating. I can just imagine God jumping around trying to explain His love in a way we would hear it. He is hugging, laughing, creating, and totally in love with you. It is possible, friend, to feel His Love without hearing His voice or speaking His language.

Passionately loving, in my opinion, is when one does something for another without expecting anything in return. One wise marriage counselor said, "Husbands and wives should not think about giving merely "50/50", they should be giving "100/100!" In other words, a relationship that will thrive is one based on giving 100% and not expecting one thing back. (Sounds crazy hard, right?)

I am just the Aunt and utterly devoted to my nieces and nephews. Imagine being their parents. They went through agony to get them and will do it again. In fact, they *DID do it again—two more times*! True saints, ya'll. It's the same with our Heavenly Father. He went through anguish and torture to bring us home. He is holy and perfect and we are not. That mere fact separates us. There had to be something to bridge the gap, something to overcome the language barrier and he provided it. He is so smitten in love with you and He demonstrated it through a cruel death. Just like me trying to act out children's stories with my niece, He acted out love by covering our un-holiness so we can be adopted into his family.

Oh my word that is Love and it is YOU He loves. Do you see it, beloved? He knows every freckle, thought, white lie, stupid joke and He is still totally, downright, absolutely and completely in love with you. Enough to die to be with you!

Chapter 14

"LET'S GET MARRIED THEN"

"Love is like air: it is invisible, but everyone needs it to live." –Author Unknown

Ah, something we all desire in the depths of our soul … to be loved. Loved in a way that makes you want to grit your teeth, or listen to Journey's "Don't Stop Believin'" all day long. What a beautiful feeling to be loved!

But what in the world does that mean?

Our English language sells us short on great verbiage. We have the same word – love –to express the joy of eating a favorite food and a mother toward her child. The same word also describes the affection of a coworker and a passionate teenaged relationship.

Love is so hard to define.

In my opinion – if you're asking – I think the word LOVE is the most over used word, yet the most desired one in our vocabulary. Hearing the words "I love you" can melt a heart, turn a rebellion, start a fight or cause a tear. Amazing how powerful this "love" is.

And yet, it goes so well in a book with the word PASSION in the title.

I always had a boyfriend. In fact, I remember having two at one time in elementary school. Yes, I was the player in 4th grade, but looking back, I quite honestly believe it was just a pure desire to be "wanted." There is a down deep yearning to feel desired, to have someone really know you whom you can be comfortable with no matter what. This physiological command begins on the first day of your life. If an infant is not touched, hugged, caressed and loved on, the baby will grow to become unable to function in society.

There are many different levels, but Reactive Attachment Disorder is real. At the most severe level, the human who has not bonded with a parent, caretaker or another human will not survive and at a lesser level, not grow physically or mentally. In the core of every cell of our body we need to be connected.

To put it simply, without human connection we will not thrive.

It's not only applicable to infants and children. Just because you have a little experience in life doesn't diminish your longing to love and be loved. What about those in nursing homes or assisted living spaces? Some may only experience human contact when they are prodded, changed, or poked. It absolutely breaks my heart that there are some people, many of them elderly, who won't be lovingly caressed, hugged or even fist bumped for days, weeks and maybe months.

As I was giving out obligatory hugs in the fellowship center at church one recent Sunday morning, one particular friend hugged me a little longer than usual. I'll admit, it was awkward and lots of things were going through my head. Was she sad? Was she upset with me? Was she having a meltdown? When she pulled back, she thanked me, "Did you realize Heidi, that hug was the only human contact I've had all week? Sorry I held on a little long."

I walked away stunned! At that time, Crystal was a 29-year-old single lady working in corporate-office-America. Her family did not live close and she was not dating. So it was true. Church for her was a lifeline to feeling included in a loving relationship.

We are created this way. Desire for love runs in every fiber of our being. We are designed to have a deep-crazy-committed-unconditional kind of love in our life.

There are always naysayers out there, so let me touch on the different kinds of love that will fulfill that deep need our soul yearns for. There are four Greek words that describe the word LOVE in the Bible: Phileo, Eros, Storge, and Agape. Yes, It's all Greek to me too! But hang in there with me.

Phileo is companionship, friendship, affection, fondness. In my opinion the Phileo type of love is more steady and constant. It's like that friend that you haven't spoken to in years but when you finally do talk, the time just disappears and it's like you saw one another the day before. Phileo will meet your basic human to human desire of love, and one could go through his entire life with Phileo love only. Does the city Philidelphia sound familiar? It's call the "City of Brotherly Love"!

Storge is a natural obligation. This type of love is mostly referred to in a family situation. A parent to a child and visa versa. As a parent, I know this love. It was absolutely NOT a choice for me. The desire to love my children was completely involuntary. This word also can depict a love for a pet. Of course, like the other types of love, you can grow this love, or you can also choose to not accept this love. Who in your life do you have a Storge type of love for?

Eros depicts erotic love. This is a fanatical type of love that burns hot then dies out. Bodies are emotionally involved. This love is based on selfish desires and what one can get out of the relationship. Although this love meets needs it will not sustain a relationship on its own. Most romantic relationships start out with this type of love and if the bond does not move to the next type of love it will not last because the partners will always be searching for personal fulfillment.

(Disclaimer: In a healthy relationship, including Agape love, Eros love can flourish!)

Lastly, Agape love refers to a desire for only the good of the one being loved. This type of love is whole-heartedly not selfish and not based on conditions. This is the most noble word for love in the Greek language and depicts a self-sacrificing kind of love, even when the one being loved is unresponsive, unkind, unlovable. This love is rare. The best example of this is when someone willingly lays down his life for another, with absolutely no gain whatsoever. It gives me chills. I have experienced this type of love and it brings me to my knees.

By no means am I a Greek scholar, but I do get excited when I learn about different words for love or actual different types of love. It totally makes sense to me! All four of these types of loves are needed, but only one will reach the deeply rooted desire to be unconditionally loved.

One of my personal experiences with love happens to be my favorite love story of all times. Marty and I met at my first coaching job. I had been on staff a year when he joined as Student Development Coordinator. He was painfully quiet and I did not have time for a "slow moving conversationalist." We were the two "singles" on staff and therefore got stuck sitting next to one another at luncheons, meetings and outings. I enjoyed his company but was relishing my life in a big city with lots of other potential male counterparts. Over the course of that year, as I dated every Tom, Dick and Harry that came through, Marty and I spent a lot of time together. I guess you can say our Phileo love was growing.

Over lunch I would pour out my woes and concerns about all the men I was seeing – he would listen and nod. Sometimes I would explain to him what I wanted in a mate – he would smile and agree. He was becoming a trusted friend.

One afternoon he walked me from campus back to my apartment. He had a softball game and was killing time before he had to be on the field. We chatted until he asked me if I was excited about moving. I wasn't. The thought of packing and moving AGAIN sounded exhausting. When I told him "No, I'm not looking forward to it." He said,

"Marry me then."

Just like that. No ring, no knee and not even a question. Just "Marry me then."

For the next 45 minutes I tried to get him to tell me he was joking. Instead he talked about how we would be perfect together. (He was finally talking and I was the silent one, my head spinning!) The craziest thing happened – my eyes were opened! I knew I would spend the rest of my life with this man.

He left to play his game, and I had a tennis date. The entire time I was on that tennis court I heard his words, "Marry me then, Heidi, we both love the Lord, we both love sports, we can do life together ... just marry me then."

We had decided to sleep on it and actually go on our first date the following evening. Right before I fell asleep the phone rang.

"The offer still stands Heidi. I will wait forever for you."

That night I stayed up planning my wedding and still had not even said "yes" yet!

Looking back now, I see that both Phileo and Storge type of love is what drew me to him. Eros love – ahem, this is not one of those books – came later. But Agape love in him was and is real. This man was and is teaching me how to love without wanting anything in return. He gives without receiving, serves without compensation and always puts others first.

Who in your life are you loving with an Agape kind of love? Anyone? Have your actions always been for personal gain?

I remember once asking a husband during a marriage counseling session "How much are you giving to your wife in this relationship?" His answer broke my heart and describes what most relationships are all about.

"I am willing to give as much as she gives."

As you pursue your passionate purpose, may I encourage you to change your perspective on love? How about loving that special someone no matter if he or she has anything to give back? And if you do not have a special someone, seek out someone who needs it!

Serve unreservedly and give without return.

Chapter 15

BE CAREFUL WHAT YOU WISH FOR

"Now faith is confidence in what we hope for and assurance about what we do not see." Hebrews 11:1

My Marty has the gift of faith. He trusts, he believes, and he is truly my inspiration. This was evident one time early in our marriage. At church one Sunday the Pastor was asking for pledges for property to build a new church building. The church desired to expand, and needed funds from the congregation in order to do so. They asked the congregation to make a pledge to give toward this cause over a year's time.

As I sat in the pew a nice little number (3-digits) came to mind. At that time, we were living on rice and beans and had NOTHING extra, so I felt my huge number was lofty and would please God. My faith-filled husband wrote down a number – a long number. As I glanced over his shoulder I think

I may have gasped (loudly). His number was MORE than one month's salary.

WHAT WAS HE THINKING?! Is he crazy? And who in the world did I marry?

Being the "supportive and loving wife," I questioned his judgment the ENTIRE ride home. I chastised him for being careless and rebuked his faith. That night was awkward and I thought through all the excuses I would give to the pastor for not giving the amount we pledged. I was simply out of my comfort zone.

We rode into work together that Monday morning. We had a 55-mile commute to and fro and I used every painful minute to explain my discontent and disagreement. In my mind, this issue was not over and we had to get it settled. Well, it was officially over when we pulled into the drive at the end of our day.

Our mailbox was at the end of our ½ mile dirt driveway. Marty pulled over so I could get the mail and, as usual, go through it as we ascended the winding, bumpy driveway. Of course my eyes went right to the envelope with the real handwriting on it – those are always fun to get. The return address was from my grandfather, who was in the VA hospital, almost in a vegetative state. (My Grandfather is a hero and his story is worth an entire book in itself). Although I had seen him, I had not had a coherent conversation with him in several years. So getting a letter from him seemed very strange.

I tore it open and a check fell onto my lap.

It was a check, from my grandfather's estate – a check that was EIGHT times more than the number my husband wrote down just one day earlier. Yep, I had chill bumps too.

This began a series of FAITH-FILLED decisions and I quickly began to see why my husband had faith. When he felt strongly that he needed to step out of his comfort zone on faith, he just did – usually with no explanation. One of my favorite quotes (I have no idea who to give credit to) goes like this:

"Whenever you are called to step out into the darkness, two things can happen – 1) you will step on solid ground, or 2) you will learn to fly!"

Many times in our marriage, Marty and I have done one or the other. We have stepped into the unknown and either took another step, or sprouted wings and flew! Time and time again we have had an opportunity to see faith be real.

After having a perfect little boy and a perfect little girl, our family felt complete. However, God wasn't finished blessing us with kids – when I went to the doctor thinking I had the flu, I came out with a positive pregnancy test! Baby number three was on the way. I was knee deep in potty training, toddler toys, sleepless nights and feeling pulled in a million different directions.

Isaac and Rhea were my life – and I was theirs. Most of the time they did NOT want daddy to dress them, feed them, bathe them. As their mommy, I was their sole-provider and I was weary. Bringing in another needy-life-sucking-being seemed daunting and completely overwhelming.

So I prayed.

I had witnessed Marty's prayers being answered as he boldly stepped out in faith, so I too asked God to intervene. "God, please let this little one LOVE her daddy. Make their relationship super strong. Give them something special. Give her a desire to be with him too, and NOT just me." It was a desperate prayer and I needed it answered!

Abby Mae was born May 23, 2006. But, little did we know, Marty would be laid off from work on May 28, 2006. Five days into his paternity leave, they asked him to come in, where they'd give him this unwelcome news. This was nowhere close to being predicted.

BUT because of this he would be home the first five months of Abby's life. Every single day he would bathe, nap, dress, hold, coddle, and build this strong bond I never thought possible. Yep, God answered my prayer – just not quite the way I intended. He showed me His faithfulness once again, yet I wanted to take control.

In usual "supportive" wife fashion, I badgered, nagged, coaxed, and shared many plans on how, when, where and why to get a job to my husband. Oh my word, I must've been a horrible resounding gong that was pure torture to be around all day. Days turned into weeks and weeks into months, and I was running low on my faith fuel.

In the fourth month of Marty's unemployment, we hit the darkness. Our mortgage was due and we were out of money. Marty was searching, interviewing, and hustling for jobs. We had been on several family interviews for a church ministry job. At one time we felt very strongly that we'd be moving to Lubbock, Texas! We were desperate and we needed answers. Yet the entire time Marty and Abby were creating this special bond, God was strengthening my faith even more.

Again, on a simple Sunday morning, Marty and I prayed for provision. We asked God to provide. After church my mom was visiting from out of town and helped make Sunday dinner. I had thrown a bag of frozen vegetables into a pot to steam. As we were setting out the dishes I scooped out the mixed veggies into a bowl to be set on the table. One particular vegetable looked a little odd to Marty so he did a further examination.

To our horror and disgust, IT WAS A FROG – well 3/4 of one! Yes, a frog in our vegetables! We were shocked! And of course we could not continue with our Sunday meal. The following morning, I called the company designated on the label to explain what I had found. Now I was NOT calling for a hand out or retribution. I was just hoping for my money back and maybe some counseling for my children because clearly they'll never eat vegetables again. The lady on the end of the phone asked if I would send the bag with the vegetables and frog to her, and for my suffering, she would love to send me and my family out to dinner and would give us $100 to do so. However, my husband –who is so NOT the confrontational type – didn't feel this adequately compensated us for such a catastrophic experience. So when all was said and done, this company would send us a check for $500!

Our mortgage payment was $502. It was due Thursday. We got the check for $500 on Wednesday. And by the next time our mortgage was due, Marty had a dream job and is still working there today, a decade later!

In my honest opinion, I truly believe that God takes care of those who trust in Him. It may be a check from a loved one, it may be a loss of a job, or it may be a frog in your vegetables. The truth is, HE cares! He wants us to know He cares. He cares and loves us so much that he provided a way for us to be with Him forever and ever.

The whole faith thing is definitely something I have to work on each and every day. The truth is, faith is basic belief without seeing, hearing, or touching. It's completely foreign to most of us. Give it a try. Cry out to the One who spoke this world into existence. Share your deepest desires to the One who knows every hair on your head.

Have faith in yourself as well. Belief is the first step. Having faith that God will provide a bountiful crop, yet you do not sow any seed is plain foolishness. Have faith and take that first step. If you want to write a book, go buy a computer and start writing. If you want to start a business, get a mentor and start working on a business plan. Even Moses had to put his foot in the water.

Yes, the very same Moses who led all the Israelites out of bondage from Egypt. Soon after they left, Egyptian rulers changed their minds and started to pursue them. Here they are – all the men, women, children and every possession they had, and they were stuck between the giant Red Sea and a mean army of Egyptians!

Moses was a man of faith. He had seen all kind of things happen. He had to believe, so he took a step. It wasn't until Moses *stepped* into the sea that GOD split the waters and provided a way for the Israelites to walk through to the other side. God didn't demonstrate His faithfulness until Moses showed his faith by taking ONE step!

Are you going to do it? Are you going to believe? Are you going to step into the unknown? It is up to you friend.

Chapter 16

UNDESERVED FAVOR

*"Therefore, since we have been justified through faith,
we have peace with God through our Lord Jesus Christ,
through whom we have gained access by faith into
this grace in which we now stand. And we boast in
the hope of the glory of God." – Romans 5:2*

When Isaac, my oldest, was about 5-years old we lived in a home we could barely afford, and I was a stay at home mom with him, and his two sisters -three and one-year old. Although I had always dreamed of being a stay-at-home mom, honestly it was not meeting my expectations and I was struggling. My selfish self needed time for me and it was no-where to be found. I'm pretty sure bathing was optional, I lived off chicken nuggets and gold fish, and my source of entertainment was a big purple dinosaur or a clown lady singing "In the Beginning God Made the heavens and the earth, and it was good"—only lyric to entire song over and over and over and … You get the picture.

My deep-hearted desire was to raise up these precious gifts from God to be perfect citizens in society. My aspiration for all three is that they would love others, make a difference in the world and impress everyone around then with their humility and smartness. That dream quickly vanished and I went into survival mode. (sorry dads, you may not get this, but every mom in the world completely understands.)

One day Isaac asked for a cookie, and just like my own diet I had re-started the vow to not give my children too much sugar. I said "no".

"Pleeeeease Mommy!"

"No baby, you don't need a cookie, have a cheese stick"

"I WANT A COOKIE!"

"Baby you don't need a cookie!"

"Yes I do!!!!!!! I NEED A COOKIE"- pretty sure he started morphing into a small incredible hulk and nothing would satisfy him except that stupid cookie.

"MOMMY MOMMY MOMMY I HATE YOU, You never give me a cookie I'm not your friend!"

You get the picture. The scene escalated for many minutes and I lost it. Instead of doing the James Dobson gentle answer thing, I picked up the cookie and hurled it like a major league pitcher across the room.

"FINE! HERE'S YOUR COOKIEEEEEEEEE!"

-Smash-

The cookie hit the wall and busted into a million pieces. Silence. I had done it. Isaac's eyes filled with puddles of water and his bottom lip started to hang out. He looked at me, then the cookie and back at me.

I had ruined my son. Broke his spirit. Took his trust in his mom and squashed like a bug. He will definitely have nightmares of me forever and probably scared to walk in my path. What have I done? My thoughts were flooded with horrible ways I damaged my son forever.

"Oh Isaac baby, mommy is so very sorry. I didn't mean to lose it like that. Can you forgive me? Isaac, honey, are you ok? ... ...

Isaac, Bubba? Are you ok?"

Sobbing as though he lost his best friend, he fell to his knees into the discarded cookie crumbs and cried,

"Mommy, --sob sob, blubber blubber--you broke my cookie."

How many times do we think our words or actions are received one way, but really taken another? Isaac, at that time, was not concerned with my lack of discipline and loss of self control. He had no clue my heart was broken by the example I set for him- his focus was that cookie—and that cookie ONLY!

We go through life unintentionally throwing daggers-or cookies-with words that cut, but are clueless to the impact they have on the one that took the blow. On the other hand, sometimes we wear our emotions on our sleeve and lose it at a comment that was meant to be uplifting.

My best friend is the most gracious person I know. She knows things about me that would cause the friendship to be ruined. She lets my unkind words, hateful attitude and jerk behavior roll off and she loves me anyway. She undeservedly passes out grace when the world would say she should push back! She not only does that with me, but all those around her. Everyone needs a friend that will let you share every hurtful thing in your heart, yet seem to forget instantly the ugliness that you spewed.

Grace, my friends--undeserved forgiveness! That is the ONLY thing that will heal broken hearts, mend destroyed relations and allow for growth. On the contrary when you do not receive grace, bitterness grows. And like my mom always said- bitterness is like a super sharp star that keeps growing in your heart. Eventually it'll start poking and hurting you, and in response you are mean, frustrated and grumpy.

Have you ever experienced a pardon? You totally deserved wrath, but for some reason was let off scot-free? Do you remember how that made you feel?

In college I drove a 1992-Candy-Red Honda Prelude, decked out with sunroof and black leather seats. I loved that car. It was my dream car. My parent's home was 81 miles down old highway 4 and if I timed it just right could make it home under an hour. That's if I didn't get pulled over.

Yes, I was a speeder. One highway patrol pulled me over 3 months in a row. After the 3rd ticket, my court appearance would be in the tune of $1300! Might as well be a million to a starving college kid—with a nice car.

That Tuesday morning, I got dressed to meet the judge and throw myself on the mercy of the court. I had planned tears, a good story, and practiced my puppy-dog eyes. Three tickets and potential license suspension caused this girl to be a nervous wreck.

"Hi, my name is Heidi Klein, I am to appear in court for multiple, uhem, speeding tickets." I squeaked at the clerk. "Just a moment." She flatly said as she pounded the keys to her computer.

"What was your name again?"

"Heidi Klein." Sweat is now dotting my upper lip.

"How do you spell that?" she asked with no emotion.

"K-L-E-I-N." oh no, it's bad, real bad, my heart was racing. I was imagining they pulled my file and was using it in some "scared-straight" talk to the younger generation.

Typing and breathing loudly the court clerk peered over her glasses to me and said,

--and I still cannot believe this happened—

"Ma'am, there is no record of you or a court date, are you sure you have the right date?" I handed her the citations and she reviewed them. Punched the keys more. The people in line behind me started rocking back and forth.

"Nope, nothing here. You're free due to a technicality. Must be your lucky day."

FREE?! What?! Technicality!!!!! I don't understand …

Pretty sure I floated out of that court house and vowed to NEVER EVER speed again!

I deserved the slammer or a fine at least! I broke the law and I should've paid! But I was pardoned. I was given a second chance. I was shown grace- undeserved favor.

How many times did I show disrespect to my parents? Or spoke shortly to my husband. I do deserve a harsh response, my action did and does warrant an unkind gesture, but I have received grace nonetheless.

When I talked to Isaac about the cookie incident I was so worried he would remember his mommy as a crazy lady with no control at all. I found that his perspective was completely different. He was concerned only for his cookie. He did not remember steam coming out of my ears or the redness of my face. Although I deserved one thing, I received another.

Undeserved Favor.

With that undeserved forgiveness I received an energy and desire to love hard, lead with boldness and passionately pursue my purpose.

That is what has happened to me spiritually. I believe the Creator of this universe created mankind. Although He is holy, He gave us a free will to choose his holiness. Well, we chose ungodliness. With that, we are eternally separated from our Creator. We deserve eternal separation from the creator. We deserve death.

However, because of His great love for us, He made a way to redeem us from our deserved punishment! He shows us undeserved favor, forgives our unholiness because His Son paid that debt. The Bible says:

"But God demonstrates His own love toward us, in that while we were yet sinners, Christ died for us." Romans 5:8

We get a pardon! Someone else paid the fine! We are rewarded when we should be condemned. This is undeserved forgiveness and should be received, passed on, and duplicated.

Whether you are finding your purpose in Leading others, finding your love or merely living life, it comes down to this: Grace. Receiving unmerited favor and showing undeserved forgiveness is, in my opinion, the most important principle in finding your passion. Without acknowledgement of this grace we will never fully find the God-given passionate purpose that is in us!

ACKNOWLEGMENTS

I am pretty sure most people will not make it back to this part of the book, however, for the faithful few I want to make sure you know you are a blessing!

YES- You the reader! Without you there would not be a book- just wasted paper and random letters. But because of you my silly stories can come to life, inspire others to do more and maybe even make you laugh or cry! So thank you so much for reading these pages. Now please do me a favor and tell someone else to read it!

Thank you to my family. Yea, yea, you hear that all the time, but I really mean it! Without you NONE of these stories would have application and it would be a real boring story to read!

To my Mom and Dad- Randy and Karen Klein-hard working ordinary folk that decided to BE PRESENT and persevere. I know there were times you wanted to give up! I know there were times you cried and didn't know how to go on! But you did. You pushed on and plowed through all of life's bumps and bruises. Most importantly, thank you for the memories. For trying to make each day precious. Thank you for M & M's in my eggs, renting a convertible in Florida, having diving contests, and wild rides on the boat. You set the bar high on living life and I truly thank God for you.

To my sister, Tammy Grinn, Oh sweet little sister. How giant can you be! You are the smart one with wisdom beyond years; the one that learned lessons from other's mistakes; the one that decided to make a difference in the world despite every critic out there (including me). I would not have faith in God, confidence to live or craving for dark chocolate without you. Thank you for being my sister and choosing to be my friend.

Thank you sweet husband, Marty McKee. Honestly have never and probably will never again meet another person like you. Each day you rise to find a way to bless me. It's crazy, and the undeserved, unconditional agape love you show is such a blessing to me and our children. I pray one day I can see me the way you see me. Thank you for loving me-marrying you is truly the best thing I ever decided to do!

Sweet kids- Isaac, Rhea and Abby, Thank you! I know it must be tough being my kids! But I thank you for hanging with me. Thank you for letting me turn every situation into a "teachable" moment. Life would absolutely stink without your hugs, kisses, snuggles and sweet words of encouragement. I pray God uses you in mighty ways as you pursue your purpose!

All the rest of the people that have pushed me, encouraged me, laughed at and with me- THANK YOU:

Nieces and Nephews, so honored to be your aunt-I love you! Church family –Centerpoint Church, Mesquite, Texas-thanks for loving us and being family to us.
Team Beloved, you are amazing.
Grandparents, Aunts, Uncles, cousins friends. Thank you so for simply loving me.

Thank you to those that helped me WRITE this! Beth Avila-you are awesome, thanks for the line editing; Cindy Hiester, thank you for your amazing feedback and being real; Tammy White, thanks for a lot of the material and helping me just be better and Karen Klein, thanks for proofreading.

NOTES

ABOUT THE AUTHOR

Heidi McKee and her husband Marty, live in Forney, Texas with their three kids (plus dogs). In addition to running a successful direct sales business, Heidi uses her passion for people speaking at events and pushing others to pursue find their passionate purpose. Heidi has also illustrated and published a scripture coloring *Beloved Words Coloring Book*

If you would like Heidi to come inspire your team, organization or ministry please reach out at

Heidimckeeministries.com
or Heidi@teambeloved.com

Printed in the United States
By Bookmasters